1 & 2

THESSALONIANS

1 & 2

THESSALONIANS

◆

H. A. IRONSIDE

Revised Edition

Introductory Notes by
John Phillips

LOIZEAUX
Neptune, New Jersey

First Edition, 1947
Revised Edition, 1997

1 & 2 THESSALONIANS
© 1997 by Loizeaux Brothers, Inc.

A Publication of Loizeaux Brothers, Inc.
*A Nonprofit Organization Devoted to the Lord's Work
and to the Spread of His Truth*

Unless otherwise indicated, Scripture quotations are taken from
the King James version of the Bible.

Profile taken from *Exploring the Scriptures*
© 1965, 1970, 1989 by John Phillips

Library of Congress Cataloging-in-Publication Data

Ironside, H. A. (Henry Allan), 1876-1951.
1 & 2 Thessalonians / H.A. Ironside. — Rev. ed. / Introductory
notes by John Phillips.
Rev. ed. of: Philippians, Colossians, Thessalonians. 1st ed. 1947.
ISBN 0-87213-414-8 (pbk.: alk. paper)
1. Bible. N.T. Thessalonians—Commentaries.
I. Ironside, H.A. (Henry Allan), 1876-1951. Philippians,
Colossians, Thessalonians. II. Title.
BS2725.3.I76 1997   96-39946
227'.8107—dc21

Printed in the United States of America
10 9 8 7 6 5 4 3 2 1

CONTENTS

A PROFILE

FIRST AND SECOND THESSALONIANS
JESUS IS COMING AGAIN

BY JOHN PHILLIPS

T
he church at Thessalonica was founded by Paul on his second missionary journey (Acts 17:1-9). Although some Jews believed, the majority of the Christians in that city were Gentiles, and those Gentiles were mostly slaves and members of the working class (1 Thessalonians 4:11-12). Paul's brief but amazingly fruitful ministry at Thessalonica was abruptly terminated by unbelieving Jews who incited a riot, obliging him to move on. He and his companions then journeyed to Berea. Driven out of Berea by persecution, Paul went on to Athens, but left Timothy and Silas behind. At Athens Paul sent word for his companions to follow him speedily, but 1 Thessalonians 3:1-2 seems to indicate that he sent Timothy back to Thessalonica to inquire about the welfare of the infant church there. In time, Timothy returned to Paul (now at Corinth) and brought with him a glowing account of the Thessalonian church (3:6). That prompted the apostle to write his first letter to the Thessalonians.

First Thessalonians

The theme of 1 Thessalonians is the second coming of Christ and its effect on believers. Each of the five chapters ends on the note of the second coming. Interestingly enough, there is not a single Old

7

Testament quotation in the Epistle, although there are Old Testament allusions, as in 5:1-3.

Paul's discussion of the Lord's coming can be outlined in terms of saving, stimulating, stabilizing, strengthening, and sanctifying truth:

I. THE LORD'S COMING: A SAVING TRUTH (1:1-10)
   A. How the Thessalonians Have Continued with the Lord (1:1-4)
   B. How the Thessalonians First Came to the Lord (1:5-10)

II. THE LORD'S COMING: A STIMULATING TRUTH (2:1-20)
   A. The Totality of Paul's Commitment (2:1-2)
   B. The Transparency of Paul's Conduct (2:3-12)
   C. The Triumph of Paul's Converts (2:13-14)
   D. The Tragedy of Paul's Countrymen (2:15-16)
   E. The Tangibility of Paul's Crown (2:17-20)

III. THE LORD'S COMING: A STABILIZING TRUTH (3:1-13)
   A. Paul's Concern (3:1-5)
   B. Paul's Comfort (3:6-11)
   C. Paul's Call (3:12-13)

IV. THE LORD'S COMING: A STRENGTHENING TRUTH (4:1-18)
   A. Our Mighty Potential (4:1-2)
   B. Our Moral Purity (4:3-8)
   C. Our Measured Progress (4:9-10)
   D. Our Manifest Purpose (4:11-12)
   E. Our Magnificent Prospects (4:13-18)

V. THE LORD'S COMING: A SANCTIFYING TRUTH (5:1-28)
   A. A Word of Explanation (5:1-13)
     1. For the Sons of Men (5:1-3)
     2. For the Saints of God (5:4-13)
   B. A Word of Exhortation (5:14-28)
     1. Walk Virtuously (5:14-15)
     2. Walk Victoriously (5:16-28)

Paul was held in tender regard by the Thessalonian believers, so he felt no need to assert his apostolic authority. The only other Epistles from which he excluded his title of apostle are 2 Thessalonians, Philippians, and Philemon. Paul began 1 Thessalonians by recalling the conversion of his Thessalonian friends and reminding them of how they had "turned to God from idols to serve the living and true God; And to wait for his Son from heaven" (1:9-10).

Next Paul reminded the Thessalonians of how careful he was when among them to behave himself in an exemplary way. He told of his joy that the Thessalonians unhesitatingly accepted the gospel at face value. Although he had been driven out of their city by Jewish troublemakers, Paul was stimulated by the thought that the Thessalonian believers would comprise his hope, his joy, and his crown of rejoicing at the Lord's coming.

Repeatedly Paul told the Thessalonians of his desire to see them again. He recounted the comfort he had received from Timothy's report and disclosed how he ceaselessly prayed that he might have another opportunity to visit Thessalonica in order to perfect that which was lacking in the faith of the new believers (3:10). He fixed their attention again on the Lord's coming as a purifying hope that could give them real stability in their Christian lives.

Next Paul reminded them that they were to remember the charges he had left with them and live as saints should. He then discussed the thrilling hope of the rapture awaiting all believers, living or dead, at the Lord's coming. This truth was to be a source of comfort and satisfaction to all.

Paul refreshed the minds of the Thessalonians concerning "the times and the seasons" connected with the Lord's return and reminded them that His coming would be a time of disaster for those left behind. Believers are "not appointed...to wrath" (5:9), but this does not mean that they can live loosely. They are to live lives of practical sanctification so that their "whole spirit and soul and body be preserved blameless unto the coming of our Lord Jesus Christ" (5:23). Far from being an abstract theological idea, the Lord's coming is one of the most practical truths found in the New Testament.

Second Thessalonians

Paul's two Thessalonian letters have much in common. Both contain important passages on the Lord's coming (1 Thessalonians 4:13-18; 2 Thessalonians 2:1-12). But there are differences. The first letter has to do mainly with the church; the second mainly with the world. The first tells of Christ's appearing in the air; the second tells of His advent to the earth. The first has to do chiefly with the day of Christ; the second chiefly with the day of the Lord.

After writing his first Epistle to the Thessalonians, Paul received further news to the effect that the believers were being shaken in their faith by deceptive teaching on the Lord's return. Someone, it appears, had caused them to be troubled by the belief that the day of the Lord had already begun (2 Thessalonians 2:2). Paul reminded the Thessalonians that he had already told them about what to expect (2:5). Two things must happen before the day of the Lord begins: there must be an apostasy and the "man of sin" must appear on the earth.

Second Thessalonians can be outlined in terms of Paul's word of admiration and his word of admonition.

I.   INTRODUCTION (1:1-2)
II.   PAUL'S WORD OF ADMIRATION (1:3-12)
    A. A Word of Undiluted Praise (1:3-4)
    B. A Word of Undisputed Promise (1:5-10)
    C. A Word of Undefeated Prayer (1:11-12)
III. PAUL'S WORD OF ADMONITION (2:1–3:15)
    A. The Greatness of the Coming Lie (2:1-12)
       1. The Immediate Deception Paul Fought (2:1-2)
       2. The Immense Deception Paul Foresaw (2:3-12)
    B. The Greatness of the Christian Life (2:13–3:15)
       1. The Believer Is Chosen (2:13-14)
       2. The Believer Is Challenged (2:15–3:5)
          a. To Trust (2:15-17)
          b. To Travail (3:1-2)
          c. To Triumph (3:3-5)
       3. The Believer Is Charged (3:6-15)
          a. The Need for Discipline (3:6-11)
          b. The Nature of Discipline (3:12-15)
IV. CONCLUSION (3:16-18)

Paul began his second letter by consoling the Thessalonians in their sufferings for the cause of Christ and by assuring them that the coming of Christ would bring ample compensation as well as a full measure of retribution for the world.

Then he turned his attention to the great "falling away" that will climax in the appearing of the "man of sin" and the consummation of the age. The last dispensation ended in the rejection of the true Christ; the present dispensation will end in the world's acceptance of the antichrist. Paul confirmed that the Restrainer (2:7) would finally be removed so that wickedness might come to its final bloom and be dealt with in judgment.

The apostle closed the second letter, as he did the first, with a practical admonition. Some believers had become so convinced that the Lord's return was to take place immediately that they had given up working for a living, thereby bringing the faith into disrepute. Paul told them plainly that the Lord's coming was not to be immediate and commanded them to get back to work. Waiting and working go hand in hand.

PREFATORY NOTE

TO FIRST EDITION

This commentary on the Thessalonian Epistles consists of expository messages that were given over a period of ten weeks on the Lord's day at the Moody Memorial Church in Chicago. The addresses were stenographically reported, but have been abbreviated somewhat by the elimination of considerable matter that was either overly repetitious or deemed not suitable for the general reader. Repetition that can hardly be avoided in addressing changing audiences would be needlessly redundant in a book, but some things are reiterated because certain truths are treated or alluded to in both Epistles. It is hoped that the shortening of the messages will not mar the effectiveness of the attempt to elucidate the great lessons that St. Paul was used of God to present to the Thessalonian church.

H. A. Ironside
February 1946

FIRST THESSALONIANS

◆

CHAPTER ONE

SERVING AND WAITING

O f all the letters that Paul wrote under the guidance of the Holy Spirit, the Thessalonian Epistles are the earliest that the Lord in His grace has preserved for the edification of the church. Evidently they were written from Corinth after persecution drove Paul from Berea. At his request, Timothy and Silas had remained behind and gone on to Thessalonica. Then they had come to Corinth to report to Paul on the condition of the young church.

According to Luke's account in the book of Acts, Paul had preached the gospel on three successive sabbaths in the Jewish synagogue at Thessalonica. How much longer he remained in the city we are not told, but it could not have been very long. The results of his short visit were remarkable. Quite a group were brought to a saving knowledge of the Lord Jesus Christ. Some of these converts were Jews, but the majority were apparently Gentiles who had been taught to see the folly of idolatry and led to put their trust in the living God as revealed in His Son.

Paul was deeply concerned about these young converts. They seemed to be like sheep without a shepherd, although of course he realized that the great Shepherd was ever watching over them. Paul told us he had no rest in his spirit while he waited for news about them because he feared that Satan might take advantage of those so recently brought to Christ. However, the report of Timothy and Silas was most encouraging and led to the writing of Paul's first letter to the Thessalonians.

Note that the second coming of our Lord Jesus Christ is referred to in some way in every chapter of this Epistle. Although the letter was addressed to babes in Christ, the apostle realized the importance of giving them clear instruction regarding this great theme.

Today we are often told that Christians need not give much thought to the doctrine of the second advent. Many ministers have no clear convictions regarding it and never preach on it at all. In the classrooms of theological seminaries this doctrine often becomes just a theme for academic discussion. But to Paul the second advent was a tremendously important and exceedingly practical truth that needed to be emphasized because of its bearing on the hearts and lives of God's beloved people.

First Thessalonians 1, which tells how the gospel was received in Thessalonica, closes with a picture of a group of happy believers earnestly serving God while waiting expectantly for the return of Jesus Christ.

Apostolic Salutation (1 Thessalonians 1:1)

Note that Paul's fellow laborers, "Silvanus, and Timotheus," are linked with him in this greeting to the young converts.

The expression "the church...which is in God the Father and in the Lord Jesus Christ" is peculiar to the Thessalonian letters. Of course it refers to the same church that is elsewhere spoken of as "the body of Christ," but here the emphasis is on the new relationship into which these young Christians had come. They were now linked in infinite grace with God the Father; they were His children. They owed their new position in the family of God to the Lord Jesus Christ, who had given Himself for them.

When Paul said, "Grace be unto you, and peace," he was not speaking of the grace that saves from judgment, but the grace that sustains from day to day. Neither was he speaking of peace *with* God; his readers had already made their peace with God. Paul was referring to the peace *of* God, which is the abiding portion of all who trust in the loving Father and seek to walk in obedience to the Lord Jesus Christ.

Paul's Prayers (1 Thessalonians 1:2-4)

In 1 Thessalonians 1:2 Paul referred to his prayers for his readers. It is remarkable how often the apostle spoke of bearing up God's people in prayer. He was a man of intense activity: preaching, visiting from house to house, often working at tentmaking for his daily bread. Yet he found time to intercede with God on behalf of all the churches that he had been used of the Lord to found. He also remembered in prayer many Christians he had not even met, as in the case of the Colossians.

In 1 Thessalonians 1:3 Paul linked the three graces about which he would later write in the Corinthian Epistle: faith, hope, and love. In Thessalonians the order is different and he spoke not simply of these graces themselves, but of the spiritual realities connected with them: the "work of faith," the "labour of love," the "patience of hope."

Faith, we are told elsewhere, "worketh by love" (Galatians 5:6). James insisted that "faith without works is dead" (James 2:20). The young Thessalonian converts showed their faith by their work.

Love, to be real, must be self-sacrificing. Therefore we read of the "labour of love." It is one thing to talk about loving our brothers, loving Israel, loving lost souls; but our love is not genuine unless we are willing to labor earnestly for the blessing of those for whom we profess to have this deep concern.

The hope of the believer is the coming of our Lord Jesus Christ. We may long for the day when trials and tribulation will be ended and Christ will take us to be with Himself, but we are not to be impatient as we await that glad consummation. Christ Himself, seated on the throne of God, is the epitome of patience. "The husbandman waiteth for the precious fruit of the earth, and hath long patience for it, until he receive the early and latter rain" (James 5:7). Thus Paul spoke of the "patience of hope."

During all the centuries since Christ ascended to Heaven, as we count time on earth, He has waited patiently for the end of the church's testimony. Then the Lord will descend in the air to call His own to be with Him, and the change that the poet has expressed will be true of all believers:

> He and I in that bright glory
> One deep joy shall share:
> Mine, to be forever with Him,
> His, that I am there!
>   (Gerhard Tersteegen)

In 1 Thessalonians 1:4 we learn that Paul prayed knowing "your election of God." How did he know this? Had he been permitted to look into eternity's books where his readers' names had been written before the foundation of the world? Had God revealed to him His divine sovereign decrees? Not at all! Paul saw in the lives of the Thessalonian believers so much evidence of the new birth that he had no question concerning their election. Paul knew that the fruit of the Spirit which he saw was not a natural gift, but the outflowing of the new life in the power of the Holy Ghost. Such evidence convinces others of our election also.

Paul's Ministry (1 Thessalonians 1:5-10)

In 1 Thessalonians 1:5-10 the apostle summarized the effects of his ministry among the Thessalonians. He began by saying in verse 5, "Our gospel came not unto you in word only, but also in power, and in the Holy Ghost, and in much assurance." The gospel of course must come in word. It is the business of the servants of Christ to proclaim the word of the truth of the gospel to a lost world. As 1 Corinthians 1:21 tells us, "It pleased God by the foolishness [simplicity] of preaching to save them that believe." But the mere statement of gospel truth, apart from the power of the Holy Spirit, is not likely to produce results like those that were seen in Thessalonica.

It is true that God in His sovereignty may use His own Word, no matter who proclaims it, or even if it is only read; He has often done so. His general method, however, is to empower devoted men to set forth the Word with clarity and in the energy of the Holy Spirit. Then the results are assured. The Lord Jesus told His disciples, "Ye shall receive power, after that the Holy Ghost is come upon you: and ye shall be witnesses unto me" (Acts 1:8). Another rendering of the verse reads, "Ye shall receive the power of the Holy Ghost coming upon you, and ye shall be witnesses unto me." The importance of speaking in the power of the Holy Spirit should never be ignored. To mistake human eloquence or oratory for preaching in the power of the Spirit of God is a great mistake. Someone has well said that "preaching is eloquence touched with fire."

In the power of the Holy Spirit, Paul and his companions proclaimed the gospel as they went from place to place. The result of their proclamation was that people were led to trust in Christ and also received "much assurance." It is a lamentable fact that a great deal of what passes for gospel preaching today would never give assurance of salvation to anyone. Sermons that are theologically correct but make no true application to the needs of the hearers, are "clear as crystal, but cold as ice," as someone has said. When the Word is preached in simplicity and in the energy of the Holy Spirit, those who believe the gospel receive the full assurance of faith.

Paul added some exceedingly significant words to 1 Thessalonians 1:5: "Ye know what manner of men we were among you for your sake." He and his companions were careful to walk before God in holiness of life and in righteousness toward their fellow men. A holy minister is a tremendous weapon in the hands of God for the pulling down of the strongholds of sin.

Ralph Waldo Emerson complained, "What you *are*...thunders so that I cannot hear what you say." What a shame that this has often been true of ministers of Christ! Integrity of life, devotedness of heart, and holiness of spirit should characterize the proclaimers of the gospel of grace.

The self-denying ways of Paul and his companions made a deep impression on the Thessalonians, for he wrote in verse 6, "Ye became followers [imitators] of us, and of the Lord." It may seem strange that he spoke here of himself before he spoke of the Lord, but we need to remember that these new believers had never heard of the Lord—and probably never would have heard of Him if Paul had not gone to them. It was what these converts had seen in Paul and his companions that had led them to be interested in the things of the Lord. Then, having trusted in Christ, they took His servants as role models and, in imitating them, were really following the Lord.

The Thessalonians had "received the word in much affliction, with joy." This sounds paradoxical and indeed it is; but the Christian may be "sorrowful, yet alway rejoicing" (2 Corinthians 6:10). The affliction to which the apostle referred may have been twofold. There was of course deep contrition as the Thessalonians recognized their sinfulness and mourned over their years of ungodliness and idolatry. Then too they knew that to decide for Christ would in many instances mean separation from loved ones, grievous misunderstandings, and even bitter persecution. But they were prepared for all this. They had counted the cost and decided that Christ would mean far more to them than temporal comfort or worldly prosperity, so they joyfully received the message that told them of sins forgiven and the hope of Heaven.

So great was the change in their lives that others soon noticed it. They were examples, we are told in 1 Thessalonians 1:7, "to all that believe in Macedonia and Achaia." Thessalonica was one of the chief cities of Macedonia; Achaia was the neighboring province. To one city after another the word went forth of what had happened in Thessalonica, where Paul had labored so earnestly. They who had been converted through his preaching became preachers themselves. No one needed to question the reality of their conversion; their lives made it evident that they were in touch with God.

The Thessalonians had experienced real conversion. First Thessalonians 1:9 tells us that they had "turned to God," and in turning to God they had turned "from idols." The words are in a different order in Acts 14:15. There in speaking to the men of Lystra, Paul said, "[We] preach unto you that ye should turn from these vanities unto the living God." The two passages are not contradictory; both suggest that conversion rests on true repentance. To repent is to change one's mind—that is, to reverse one's attitude. And so the Thessalonians who had been idolaters turned to the true and living God. They were through with idolatry. Today when men trust in Christ and bow before God in repentance, they turn from the things of a godless world and yield themselves to the One who died to redeem them.

Following the conversion of the Thessalonians, they had a new attitude: they were motivated to "serve" and "wait" (these two words from 1 Thessalonians 1:9-10 cover the whole Christian life). They sought to serve the living and true God while they waited for His Son from Heaven. We are sometimes told that focusing on the second coming of the Lord has a tendency to throttle Christian activity. It is said that people with such a focus can become dreamers who are sidetracked with prophetic questions and are no longer interested in living for God and seeking to win others for Christ. Frankly my own experience teaches me that the contrary is true. My observation is that the more this blessed truth grips a man's soul, the more concerned he is about serving God and winning others to Christ. This was true of the young Thessalonian believers. They lived day by day in the expectation of Christ's return. They looked for Him—the risen and ascended One—to come back again as their Deliverer from "the wrath to come."

The wrath referred to here, I think, is not eternal judgment. From that wrath, believers have already been delivered. Paul was referring to the wrath that will come upon the world. Evidently the apostle had intimated to the Thessalonians that such a time of trouble is coming, but he had also told them that Jesus will come to snatch His own away before this wrath is let loose.

The Lord has promised to come for His own before the trumpets of this wrath begin to sound and the judgments of the great tribulation fall upon the world. His coming for His own is still the hope of His saints.

CHAPTER TWO
A CHRISTLIKE MINISTRY

Review of Ministry (1 Thessalonians 2:1-12)

In these twelve verses the apostle reviewed the ministry that he and his companions had in the city of Thessalonica. He reminded the believers how he had come to them from Philippi, where he had been "shamefully entreated" (1 Thessalonians 2:2). In Acts 16 we find the record of that shameful treatment and we learn that Paul and Silas were unjustly arrested, beaten with thongs, and cast into a dungeon where their feet were put in the stocks.

That night in the prison they prayed and sang praises unto God. Someone has said that the gospel entered Europe in a sacred concert! There were two artists: one was Paul and the other Silas—possibly a tenor and a bass. What hymns they sang we are not told, but the concert was given and it was so effective that it brought down the house. There was a great earthquake and down came the jail. That was the result of the first gospel concert of which we have any record in the New Testament. The jailer was converted.

The following day the city authorities wanted to release Paul and Silas, but Paul said, "They have beaten us openly uncondemned, being Romans, and have cast us into prison; and now do they thrust us out privily?" So that no dishonor might be connected with the gospel message, Paul refused to leave the prison inconspicuously. He demanded, "Let them come themselves and fetch us out" (Acts 16:37). The magistrates eventually agreed to come.

When Paul and Silas were released from prison, they left Philippi after a farewell meeting with the brethren in Lydia's house. The two missionaries went on down the highway to the city of

25

Thessalonica and there preached the word, and many were brought to a saving knowledge of the Lord Jesus Christ.

In 1 Thessalonians 2:3 the apostle mentioned the holiness of life that should characterize the one who proclaims the message of God. Paul was very careful about his own life. He was able to say, "For our exhortation was not of deceit, nor of uncleanness, nor in guile." He and his companions were perfectly open about everything. They had no hidden schemes. They did not go out preaching in order to make money. Their purpose was to exalt Christ and win souls.

The man who preaches the gospel should live the gospel. In his life there should be nothing unclean, no secret evil, nothing that grieves the Holy Spirit of God. If he makes personal gain his object, his ministry becomes obnoxious to God. Of course ministers of Christ have to live and the Bible says, "They which preach the gospel should live of the gospel" (1 Corinthians 9:14). But when ministers preach Christ simply as a means of earning a living, they have missed their path altogether. The Lord will support those who faithfully carry on His work.

Paul repudiated any selfish motive in his own preaching. He said, "As we were allowed of God to be put in trust with the gospel" (1 Thessalonians 2:4). That is a striking expression. The ministry is not man's choice; it is God's choice. Paul looked on this business of preaching the gospel as a privilege that God permitted him to have.

Notice that Paul and his companions were entrusted with the *gospel.* That is the one great message which the servant of Christ has to give to a lost world. People suggest all kinds of themes to ministers—and a minister of Christ should be interested in everything that is for the betterment of mankind. But his business is to preach the gospel and the Word of the Lord. If we can get men saved, everything else will soon be straightened out. If we can get men right with the Lord, there will be no trouble with other things.

And so Paul's intention was not to give political addresses or scientific lectures. He had but one desire: that men might know the gospel of the grace of God. "I determined," he said to the Corinthians,

"not to know any thing among you, save Jesus Christ, and him crucified" (1 Corinthians 2:2).

Notice how strongly the apostle spoke in 1 Thessalonians 2:5-6
about his single-hearted devotion to God. Paul and his companions
were absolutely free of selfish motives. They did not think primari-
ly of their own welfare; they thought of the welfare of others and
the glory of God. Every missionary and every minister of Christ
should have the same attitude.

Verse 7 should be translated, "We were gentle among you, even
as a nurse cherisheth her *own* children." There might be a difference in the way a nurse would treat someone else's children and the
way she would treat her own children. Paul looked on the
Thessalonian believers, these young Christians who had so recently
come to know Christ, as his own children in the faith. He exerted
himself in every possible way to build them up in Christ.

Paul might have said to his children in the faith, "Now that you
are converted, the least you can do is to be concerned about my
support." But he would not bring the gospel down to that low level.
On many occasions when he came to the end of his financial re-
sources, he turned to tentmaking in order to provide for himself and
his companions. When the saints realized their responsibility and
counted it a privilege to care for Paul, he was willing to accept their
support, but he never put them to the test.

In verses 8-9 Paul reminded the Thessalonians of his affection
for them and of his "labour and travail" on their behalf. The word
"travail" refers to the pangs of childbirth. Paul used the same word
when he wrote to the Galatians, "My little children, of whom I travail in birth again until Christ be formed in you" (Galatians 4:19).
Oh, if we only knew more of this agony of soul that characterized
Paul! If we knew more of his earnest purpose to bring people to
Christ, we might see many more confess His name. We tend to take
things in such a matter-of-fact way. It was otherwise with Paul. He
suffered if people did not come to Christ because he felt responsible for them. And he cared for young converts "as a father doth
his children" (1 Thessalonians 2:11). He followed Christ so that
they might see in him what it meant to be a true servant of the Lord.

Result of Ministry (1 Thessalonians 2:13-16)

Paul reminded the Thessalonians of the result of his work among them. Note what the gospel had done for them. Because they had seen evidence of the reality of the gospel in Paul's life, they had felt constrained to listen to his message. As they had listened, the message had reached their hearts and convicted their consciences, and they had believed it.

When they became Christians, they received the gospel not as "the word of men," but as "the word of God," and it worked effectively in them (1 Thessalonians 2:13).By the word of the gospel we are brought to repentance, and by that word the Thessalonians were regenerated, "being born again...by the word of God, which liveth and abideth forever" (1 Peter 1:23). The word of the gospel brings the message home to the hearts and consciences of men, and by that same truth they are sanctified. Jesus prayed, "Sanctify them through thy truth: thy word is truth" (John 17:17).

This truth led the Thessalonians to take a stand for Christ. Those who were Jewish by birth had to turn away from their loved ones; they had to turn away from their dearest friends, endure bitter persecution, and bear the reproach of Christ. Those who were from heathen backgrounds suffered at the hands of their heathen relatives and former friends, just as the Christian Jews in Judea suffered at the hands of their Jewish friends and relatives.

When men's eyes are blinded to the truth, there is no limit to what their religious prejudice will cause them to do. The unconverted Jews tried to hinder the apostle Paul from going to the Gentiles with the message of salvation through faith in Christ, and thus gave evidence that the wrath of God had come upon them. God is going to deal with those who reject His Son and seek to hinder those who believe in Him.

Reward of Ministry (1 Thessalonians 2:17-20)

The apostle expressed the earnest desire of his heart to see the young Thessalonian converts again. Whether or not he saw them again on earth, he could look forward with joy to meeting them at the judgment seat of Christ.

Paul wanted to go back to Thessalonica, "but Satan hindered" (1 Thessalonians 2:18) by stirring up persecutions against him. All the efforts of the devil would have accomplished nothing, however, if God had not permitted him to work. When there are obstacles in our way and we wonder whether it is Satan or God who is hindering us, we need to distinguish between God's direct will and His permissive will. Very often people suffer at the hands of Satan and his emissaries, but only if God has given His permission. We may therefore take all suffering as from God Himself.

Even if Paul never got back to Thessalonica, he would see his converts on the day when the Lord returns. They would be his crown of rejoicing, his abundant reward for his preaching, self-sacrifice, and devotion.

The souls we lead to Christ make up our crown of rejoicing. Will you not be sad if, when you meet the Lord, you have no crown of rejoicing because you have failed to lead someone to Him on earth? Have you ever talked to people about your Savior? Have you written friends letters to tell them how the Lord has saved you? Have you given the gospel message to anyone? If you have never led anyone to Christ, determine by the grace of God to point someone to the Savior who means so much to you.

Oh, the joy of winning men, women, and little children to Christ! When we stand in His presence, how precious it will be to be able to say, "Behold I and the children which God hath given me" (Hebrews 2:13). What a host will surround the apostle Paul on that day!

CHAPTER THREE
ESTABLISHED IN THE FAITH

Timothy's Mission (1 Thessalonians 3:1-5)

In Acts 16 we read of Paul's visit to Philippi. Because of persecution there, he went on to Thessalonica, where he did a great work in a short time (17:1-4). However, persecution broke out there too and the brethren sent Paul to Berea (17:5-10). In Berea he found a company of open-minded Jews who were ready to listen to the gospel and walk in the light of the Scriptures. Referring to the Bereans, Acts 17:11-12 says: "These were more noble than those in Thessalonica, in that they received the word with all readiness of mind, and searched the scriptures daily, whether those things were so. Therefore many of them believed."

These Bereans are good models for all of us because sometimes we hear ideas that are new to us and without investigation reject what we have heard. But in 1 Thessalonians 5:21 Paul told us to "prove all things; hold fast that which is good." Holy Scripture of course is the test we are to use. No matter what doctrine is taught, we are to compare it with the Word of God: if the doctrine is compatible with Scripture, we are to accept it; if the doctrine is contrary to Scripture, we are just as responsible to reject it.

The Jews who had resisted Paul at Thessalonica came down to Berea and "stirred up the people" (Acts 17:13). So the Berean brethren sent Paul to Athens, but Paul left Silas and Timothy behind (17:14-15). We are not told in the book of Acts that Paul asked them to return to Thessalonica to check on the progress of the young converts there, but we learn from 1 Thessalonians 3 that when Paul went on to Athens, he sent Timothy to Thessalonica. Because the apostle was concerned about the Thessalonians, he remained in Athens alone so that Timothy could find out whether the young converts were making progress or becoming discouraged.

I always revel in the delightful way Paul referred to his co-workers. Notice what he wrote in 1 Thessalonians 3:2: "Timotheus, our brother, and minister of God, and our fellowlabourer in the gospel of Christ." What more could be said of any servant of the Lord? A beloved brother in Christ, a dear fellow laborer—Timothy was all this to Paul. So he sent Timothy to establish and comfort the young Christians in Thessalonica.

They needed comfort because they were in the midst of a godless, pagan world. It meant a great deal in those days to make a public confession of faith in Christ. Sometimes it does not seem to mean so much now, and yet we find people afraid to take this step. The Thessalonians who came to Christ out of idolatry were surrounded by bitter enemies; yet these Christians surrendered their lives to the Lord and were a bright testimony for Him.

Paul was concerned about the possibility that they would become discouraged, so he sent Timothy to exhort them "that no man should be moved by these afflictions" (1 Thessalonians 3:3). Afflictions were to be expected: "For yourselves know that we are appointed thereunto." All Christians should expect to suffer afflictions in this world. Yet when trouble and sorrow come, how often Christians wonder if they have made a mistake. They wonder whether God has actually forgiven their sins. They wonder if they are really born again. But hear the word of the apostle: "Verily, when we were with you, we told you before that we should suffer tribulation; even as it came to pass, and ye know" (3:4). Our Lord Jesus said to His disciples before He went away, "These things I have spoken unto you, that in me ye might have peace. In the world ye shall have tribulation: but be of good cheer; I have overcome the world" (John 16:33). Acts 14:22 records Paul's teaching "that we must through much tribulation enter into the kingdom of God."

Do not be discouraged, dear suffering Christians. Do not question your Father's love because you are passing through sorrows or facing disappointing circumstances. The apostle Peter said, "Ye are in heaviness through manifold temptations: That the trial of your faith, being much more precious than of gold that perisheth, though it be tried with fire, might be found unto praise and honour and glory at the appearing of Jesus Christ" (1 Peter 1:6-7).

Paul did not want his work in Thessalonica to "be in vain" (1 Thessalonians 3:5). There is always the possibility that people will make a Christian profession without genuine repentance and implicit faith in Christ. Sometimes it is easy to go along with the crowd when many are turning to the Lord. It is easy under such circumstances to make a profession when no real work of God has been done in the soul. Paul feared that there might be some in Thessalonica who had made a profession of Christ, but were not truly regenerated. So he sent Timothy to find out if their faith was genuine.

Timothy's Report (1 Thessalonians 3:6-10)

We can imagine what it must have meant to Paul to be in Athens in utter loneliness for some time. As he walked about the streets of that great city, his heart was stirred by the idolatry he saw. An ancient Greek writer said, "In Athens it is easier to find a god than a man." Evidences of idolatry were everywhere, but not a single light was shining for Christ until Paul entered the city. He did not find much interest in the gospel until he was urged to go up to Mars Hill, where he gave the address recorded in Acts 17:22-31.

All the while Paul was witnessing in Athens, he was anxious about the young Christians at Thessalonica, but when Timothy brought a good report, it gladdened Paul's heart. Timothy spoke of their "faith and charity [love]" (1 Thessalonians 3:6) and reported that they were progressing beautifully. The Thessalonians were living for God; in fact many had become preachers. Paul was "comforted" by the good news (3:7).

Because he was so definitely linked in spirit with these young converts, he said, "Now we live, if ye stand fast in the Lord" (3:8). Every real soul-winner knows something of the meaning of those words. When we have the privilege of bringing sinners to Christ, it cheers the heart, but what a joy it is to learn afterward that they are maintaining a bright, consistent testimony! Likewise Paul's soul was refreshed and exuberant when he received the good news about the Thessalonian believers.

Young believers sometimes imagine that those who are older and act as guides and teachers are too severe if they warn about worldly things that militate against a real Christian testimony. But the love of God in the hearts of those leaders is so fervent that sometimes they have to say very strong things in order to impress on the young the importance of being wholly yielded to Christ. Let me assure you that when we stand at the judgment seat of Christ, no one will be sorry because he was completely yielded to the Lord. On that day there will be many who would give worlds, if they possessed them, to have another chance to be more devoted, more truly separated from the world, more out-and-out for their Savior in this world. Total commitment is what Paul wanted to see in his converts; it is what all faithful ministers of Christ—all soul-winners, all who have pastoral hearts—long to see in those who profess faith in His name.

Paul opened his heart to the Thessalonians. Preaching the gospel was not merely a profession. He did not go to a town, hold a series of meetings, and forget his converts when he moved on to another town. He carried his converts in his heart and always hoped to return to give them additional instruction in the faith and lead them farther along in the ways of Christ. He remembered them in prayer "night and day" (1 Thessalonians 3:10). He prayed that they might continue in the will of God and that as the truth was explained to them, they might learn to walk faithfully.

Paul's Desire (1 Thessalonians 3:11-13)

In verses 11 to 13 Paul expressed his prayerful desire for these young Christians. His words can be looked on as a prayer for every Christian from Paul's day until the end of this dispensation.

First Thessalonians 3:13 speaks of the time when we will be "unblameable in holiness." The apostle did not say, or even suggest, that we will reach that desired goal in this world. As long as we are here on earth, there will always be higher heights to reach and deeper depths to sound; there will always be sins over which we will need to have victory. But it is the will of God that by prayer we continue to make progress until at last we stand before our blessed Lord at the judgment seat. We will reach the goal "at the coming of our Lord Jesus Christ with all His saints."

We have already noted that the second coming of the Lord is presented in some aspect in each chapter of this Epistle. The first chapter tells us how the Thessalonians had turned from idols "to serve the living and true God; And to wait for his Son" (1:9-10). They lived in constant expectation of the return of the Lord Jesus Christ from Heaven. That was their daily attitude and it should be our attitude also. When we rise in the morning we should say, "The Lord Jesus may be back before night." When we commit ourselves to God before going to bed, we should remind ourselves, "Before morning comes we may hear His voice and see His face."

The second chapter tells us that all those whom we win to Christ will be our crown of rejoicing when the Lord returns to call His saints to be with Himself. All of us who are believers (no unsaved people will be present) will stand before the judgment seat and all our works will be evaluated. Everything that was of God—everything that was the result of the Spirit's working in and through us, everything that was in accordance with the will of God—will bring its reward. The reward is pictured as a crown: the crown of life for those who have suffered for Christ's sake; the crown of righteousness for those who loved His appearing; the crown of glory for those who fed the sheep of His flock; the incorruptible crown for those who pressed on steadfastly in the Christian race; and the crown of rejoicing for those who won souls. The Thessalonian believers will be included in Paul's crown of rejoicing. He will see gathered at the judgment seat all those whom he led to Christ. Then, as the third chapter tells us, they will be established and "unblameable in holiness before God."

Until that great day we are to press on; we are to put away every known sin and purge our lives of all filthiness. If someone says, "I have already attained perfect holiness," he is simply deceiving himself, for Scripture says, "If we say that we have not sinned, we make him a liar, and his word is not in us" (1 John 1:10). Holiness will not be attained until we meet our Savior, gaze on His face, and in that glorious moment become like Him. As 1 John 3:2 says, "When he shall appear, we shall be like him; for we shall see him as he is."

CHAPTER FOUR

RESPONSIBILITIES AND RAPTURE

Exhortations (1 Thessalonians 4:1-12)

In this section the apostle set forth the walk that pleases God. During his ministry among the Thessalonians, Paul had been careful to emphasize the practical side of Christianity. Sometimes we are apt to neglect this. We are so taken up with doctrine that we do not sufficiently stress our responsibilities as believers. Both sides of Christianity are important.

There is a special warning in this passage against sins of impurity. In Paul's day, immorality was so common among the heathen that even Christians were apt to look on it with a measure of indifference or even complacency. As Alexander Pope wrote:

> Vice is a monster of so frightful mien,
> As to be hated needs but to be seen;
> Yet seen too oft, familiar with her face,
> We first endure, then pity, then embrace.

Among pagan nations the vilest kind of lasciviousness was connected with the worship of their false gods. But our God is infinitely holy and we who know Him are called to be careful to avoid every tendency to uncleanness. Thus the apostle wrote, "This is the will of God, even your sanctification, that ye should abstain from fornication" (1 Thessalonians 4:3).

We often find this verse quoted in part, particularly by those who misunderstand the meaning of sanctification. They think of sanctification as a second definite work of grace that follows justification.

Building on a false premise, they attempt to find Scriptural support in the first part of this verse. But what Paul was saying was that God's will is for believers to walk in separation from all that is vile and immoral. The Thessalonians were to separate themselves from the lasciviousness and licentiousness that had characterized many of them before they were saved.

It is the will of God that believers walk in purity, looking on their bodies as devoted to Him (see Paul's exhortation in 4:4-5). Some people might say, "We live in a civilized land where men have learned the difference between clean and unclean living; we do not need an exhortation such as this." But anyone who is aware of actual conditions inside and outside the professing church realizes how relevant the admonition is. There is always the temptation to lower the Christian standard. We need to be constantly reminded of the importance of living pure lives.

It is impossible to sin in the manner of which Paul wrote without wronging others. The sins he mentioned here cannot be committed alone and other people are always injured by such unholy deeds. The apostle therefore gave the warning "that no man go beyond and defraud his brother in any matter" (4:6).

The believer's body is the temple of the Holy Spirit and it is to be devoted to the glory of our blessed Lord. If a man despises such an admonition, he "despiseth not man, but God, who hath also given unto us his holy Spirit" (4:8).

In 1 Thessalonians 4:9-10 Paul referred to that love which is the evidence of the new nature given to all who are born of God. The brotherly love of the young Thessalonian converts was obvious to all, but the apostle told them that in this (as in every other grace) there should be continuous progress.

Paul went on to give another very practical word of advice: "Study to be quiet, and to do your own business" (4:11). The word translated "study" here means "to be ambitious." We are to be ambitious to do our own business; that is, we are to mind our own business! Many people seem to have the ambition to mind any business except their own, but minding other people's business always results in strife and dissension.

When Paul exhorted the Thessalonians "to work with your own hands," he was saying that the Christian is not to be dependent on others. He is to earn his own living by honest work; if possible he is to be self-supporting. He is not to expect other people to maintain him in idleness.

The Second Coming (1 Thessalonians 4:13-18)

Following the exhortations in verses 1-12, the apostle turned to another matter, a question that was troubling the young Christians in Thessalonica. Timothy had informed Paul that they were concerned about some of their number who had died. Those who remained alive wondered, *What will happen to the departed ones when Christ comes again?*

When Paul was with the Thessalonians, he told them that Jesus was coming again to set up His kingdom on this earth, and they leaped to the conclusion that those who died before the Lord's return might not share in His reign, that only those who were living when He returned would welcome Him and have a part in the kingdom. After all, how could people who were no longer in this world reign with Him here? The apostle wrote verses 13-18 to correct their misunderstanding and share the new revelation that the Lord had unfolded to him.

Paul started, "I would not have you to be ignorant, brethren, concerning them which are asleep" (4:13). When he used the expression "asleep," he meant "dead." Later when he spoke of Jesus, he used the expression "died," but when he spoke of believers, he used the expressions "sleep" and "asleep." Christ died; He went into death and all that it involved when He took our place on the cross. But we who trust in Him will never see death. If we enter the realm of what we call "death," our bodies will just be asleep until the Lord Jesus returns. Our spirits will leave our bodies and go to be with Christ: "Absent from the body...present with the Lord" (2 Corinthians 5:8).

Paul did not rebuke believers for sorrowing when they lose their loved ones in Christ, but he did tell them not to sorrow as others do who will have no reunion at the coming of our Lord Jesus Christ.

We have the hope of reunion "if we believe that Jesus died and rose again" (1 Thessalonians 4:14)—and we do believe it! We are not Christians if we do not. The fact of Jesus' death and resurrection is the foundation truth of Christianity.

First Corinthians 15:3-4 tells us "that Christ died for our sins according to the scriptures; And that he was buried, and that he rose again the third day according to the scriptures." And Romans 4:25, referring to Christ, says, "Who was delivered for our offences, and was raised again for our justification." The body of Jesus came up from the tomb. In that body He ascended into Heaven and in that body He now sits on the throne of God.

Romans 10:9-10 states, "If thou shalt confess with thy mouth the Lord Jesus, and shalt believe in thine heart that God hath raised him from the dead, thou shalt be saved. For with the heart man believeth unto righteousness; and with the mouth confession is made unto salvation." Anyone who does not believe in the death and resurrection of Christ has no right to the name *Christian.*

In the King James version the second part of 1 Thessalonians 4:14 reads, "Them also which sleep in Jesus will God bring with him." A better translation might be, "Them which have been put to sleep by Jesus will God lead forth with Him." The blessed Lord Himself takes His weary saints and puts them to sleep until that glorious resurrection morning when they will be awakened at the sound of His voice. Then God will lead them forth with Him.

How can the Lord Jesus come with all His saints to establish His kingdom if some of His saints are in Heaven and some of them are on earth? Paul explained that when the Lord comes for His own, He will raise the dead and change the living and they will "be caught up together...in the clouds, to meet the Lord in the air" (4:17). Then God will lead them forth with the Lord Jesus when He descends in power and glory.

It was a new revelation ("This we say unto you by the word of the Lord") that we who are alive when the Lord returns will not precede those who are "asleep" (4:15). I cannot find one word in the three synoptic Gospels (Matthew, Mark, and Luke) about this aspect of the Lord's coming for His saints. In the Synoptics the coming of the Son of God with His saints to set up His kingdom on earth is always in view. The Gospel of John, however, provides a link to 1 Thessalonians 4:13-18. John told us that before the Lord went away, He said to the apostles in the upper room, "I go to prepare a place for you. And if I go and prepare a place for you, I will come again, and receive you unto myself; that where I am, there ye may be also" (John 14:2-3). They knew He was coming again to set up His kingdom; He had told them that before. But now He gave them information about a secret that He had kept in His heart until this time: "I will come again, and receive you unto myself." It is this aspect of His coming that was given by revelation to the apostle Paul and through him to us.

There will be a generation of Christians living on the earth in their natural bodies when the Lord comes again. We have no way of knowing when this blessed event will take place. It might please Him to defer His coming until we have left this world, but we are to live in daily expectation of His return.

The King James version states, "We which are alive and remain unto the coming of the Lord shall not *prevent* them which are asleep" (1 Thessalonians 4:15, italics added). The meaning of the English word "prevent" has changed in the last three hundred or more years. When the Bible was translated in 1611, *to prevent* meant "to go before." When David was speaking of his morning prayer in Psalm 119:147, he said, "I prevented the dawning of the morning." He did not mean that he prevented the sun from rising; he meant that he was up and praying before the sun rose. Today *to prevent* means "to hinder." But Paul meant that we who are alive when Christ returns will not enter the kingdom one moment ahead of those who have died. We will all go in together.

First Thessalonians 4:16 indicates that "the Lord himself shall descend from heaven." I like those words: *the Lord Himself!* He is the One for whom I am waiting! The angels said, "This same Jesus, which is taken up from you into heaven, shall so come in like manner as ye have seen him go into heaven" (Acts 1:11). It is the Lord Himself for whom we look.

He will descend "with a shout, with the voice of the archangel."

The archangel in the Old Testament is connected with the Jewish people in a very special way. Daniel 12:1 states, "At that time shall Michael stand up, the great prince which standeth for the children of thy people." The voice of Michael the archangel will be heard at the same time that the Lord gives His awakening shout. When Christ comes, the saints of all past ages as well as the saints of this age will be included in the fulfillment of prophecy.

When "the trump of God" sounds, "the dead in Christ shall rise first." The last clause can be literally translated, "The dead in Christ will *stand up* first." Millions whose bodies are sleeping in the earth will hear His voice. Lazarus heard it when he was in the tomb, and he immediately sprang to life. So all the saved who have died will stand up, come back to life, in the first resurrection.

Then we whose bodies are still alive will be "caught up together with them in the clouds" (1 Thessalonians 4:17). The definite article before "clouds" obscures the meaning of Paul's words. I do not think we are going to ascend to the fleecy clouds above our earth. Even our airmen go higher than that. But there will be so many millions of us that we will go up in clouds of people. This event is what we call the rapture of the church. We will be rapt (carried) away "to meet the Lord in the air." The word translated "meet" means "to go out to meet one in order to return with him" as in Acts 28:15.

We will be "caught up *together*" (italics added). We have fellowship together down here. We work together here under our Lord's authority. And when He returns we will be "caught up together." We will know those with whom we go to meet the Lord. Sometimes people ask me, "Will we know one another in Heaven?" We will know as we have never known before! "Then shall I know even as also I am known" (1 Corinthians 13:12). We will know as God Himself has known us.

There are wonderful events to be unfolded in the ages to come. We will stand before the Lord's judgment seat in our glorified bodies to receive rewards for the deeds done in this life. He will descend to take His kingdom; and like the armies of Revelation 19:14 following the rider on the white horse, we will come with the Lord to share in His glory on that triumphal day. This is our hope; this is the hope of the church.

But whatever events unfold, we will always be with the Lord: "So shall we ever be with the Lord." And the apostle said to "comfort one another with these words" (1 Thessalonians 4:18). Do they bring comfort to your heart? They should if you are living for Him. If you are not, there will be no comfort in "these words" for you.

CHAPTER FIVE
JUDGMENT AND COMFORT

The Day of the Lord (1 Thessalonians 5:1-11)

After unfolding the truth concerning the rapture, the apostle turned his attention to the day of the Lord. Following the rapture of the saints, the world will experience the darkest period it has ever known. In many places in the Old Testament this period is referred to as the day of the Lord or the time of trouble. It is called the great tribulation in both the Old and New Testaments. Paul referred to that day in 1 Thessalonians 5:1-2:

> Of the times and the seasons, brethren, ye have no need that I write unto you. For yourselves know perfectly that the day of the Lord so cometh as a thief in the night.

Here we see that the subject of the day of the Lord is included in the expression "the times and the seasons." Prophetic times and seasons never have to do with the Lord's coming for His church. They always have to do with events preceding and culminating in the Lord's coming to set up His kingdom here on the earth. Any attempt to figure out the time when the Lord will return for His own leads to confusion.

The expression "the times and the seasons" occurs twice elsewhere in the Scriptures: once in the book of Daniel and once in the book of Acts. In Daniel 2:19-22 we are told:

> Then was the secret [concerning Nebuchadnezzar's dream] revealed unto Daniel in a night vision. Then Daniel blessed the God of heaven. Daniel answered and said, Blessed be the name

of God for ever and ever: for wisdom and might are his: And he changeth the times and the seasons: he removeth kings, and setteth up kings: he giveth wisdom unto the wise, and knowledge to them that know understanding: He revealeth the deep and secret things: he knoweth what is in the darkness, and the light dwelleth with him.

Clearly here "the times and the seasons" had to do with events on the earth. God changes times and seasons when He postpones judgment because a nation has repented and turned to God. For example Jonah was commanded to go to Nineveh and announce that judgment would fall in forty days, but Nineveh repented and God put off her destruction for two centuries. Then judgment fell because of her further rejection of the Word of the Lord. God dealt in the same way with Israel and Judah on various occasions—He postponed judgment when they repented.

In Acts 1:6 the disciples asked the risen Savior, "Lord, wilt thou at this time restore again the kingdom to Israel?" They were speaking of the time predicted in the Old Testament. Jesus replied:

It is not for you to know the times or the seasons, which the Father hath put in his own power. But ye shall receive power, after that the Holy Ghost is come upon you: and ye shall be witnesses unto me both in Jerusalem, and in all Judaea, and in Samaria, and unto the uttermost part of the earth (1:7-8).

Nothing could be plainer than the Lord's words. Our business is not to know when the day of the Lord will begin. Our business is to preach the gospel. We are to go from people to people and from nation to nation until the entire world has heard the good news.

So we have the Old Testament predictions, Christ's words regarding the day of the Lord, and Paul's reminder that it will come "as a thief in the night" (1 Thessalonians 5:2).

Paul did not need to write to the Thessalonians about the day of the Lord because it has to do with "the times and the seasons" and therefore cannot begin while the church is still in the world. Let me emphasize that in 1 Thessalonians 5:2 Paul was not referring, as some have supposed, to the descent of the Lord in the air to call His church away. He was referring to the coming of the Lord in visible glory to set up His kingdom. The day of the Lord has to do with events that will take place after the rapture of the church and prior to the revelation of the Lord in judgment. Some Old Testament Scriptures make this clear. In Amos 5:18-20, for example, we read:

> Woe unto you that desire the day of the Lord! to what end is it for you? the day of the Lord is darkness, and not light. As if a man did flee from a lion, and a bear met him; or went into the house, and leaned his hand on the wall, and a serpent bit him. Shall not the day of the Lord be darkness, and not light? even very dark, and no brightness in it?

Some people in Israel were looking forward to the day of the Lord, for they thought that then their troubles would be over. But for them the prophet predicted woe. He said that the day of the Lord would mean fleeing from one danger only to encounter a greater one. As we would say, they would be jumping from the frying pan into the fire. The day of the Lord will be a time of judgment. God will deal with apostate Israel as well as the Gentiles because of their folly and sin. In that sense the day of the Lord is not to be desired by those who are still living in their sins. It will bring judgment and sore distress for the people still living on the earth.

Zephaniah 1:14-15 gives us a somber picture of the conditions that will prevail in the day of the Lord:

> The great day of the Lord is near, it is near, and hasteth greatly, even the voice of the day of the Lord: the mighty man shall cry there bitterly. That day is a day of wrath, a day of trouble and distress, a day of wasteness and desolation, a day of darkness and gloominess, a day of clouds and thick darkness.

In Joel 2:1-3 we read:

> Blow ye the trumpet in Zion, and sound an alarm in my holy mountain: let all the inhabitants of the land tremble: for the day

of the Lord cometh, for it is nigh at hand; A day of darkness and of gloominess, a day of clouds and of thick darkness, as the morning spread upon the mountains: a great people and a strong; there hath not been ever the like, neither shall be any more after it, even to the years of many generations. A fire devoureth before them; and behind them a flame burneth: the land is as the garden of Eden before them, and behind them a desolate wilderness; yea, and nothing shall escape them.

Joel's words remind us of the words of our Lord Jesus in Matthew 24:21-22:

Then shall be great tribulation, such as was not since the beginning of the world to this time, no, nor ever shall be. And except those days should be shortened, there should no flesh be saved: but for the elect's sake those days shall be shortened.

In view of the terrible events that have taken place so recently, we should not have any difficulty believing these prophecies. Ever since the discovery and use of the atomic bomb it has been easy to see that another world war might entail the destruction of all flesh. When the Lord referred to the elect, He had in mind the remnant in Israel and those of the nations who will be waiting for the Lord during the great tribulation.

Turning again to the Old Testament, we read in Jeremiah 30:7: "Alas! for that day is great, so that none is like it: it is even the time of Jacob's [Israel's] trouble; but he shall be saved out of it." God will have on the earth a remnant from Israel who will turn to the Lord and He will use them as witnesses to the Gentile world. As a result, many people will be prepared to welcome the Lord when He descends to take His kingdom.

Malachi 4:1-2 tells us that the ungodly Gentile world and apostate Judaism will all be destroyed in the day of the Lord, but those who turn to the Lord will be saved from destruction:

Behold, the day cometh, that shall burn as an oven; and all the proud, yea, and all that do wickedly, shall be stubble: and the day that cometh shall burn them up, saith the Lord of hosts, that it shall leave them neither root nor branch. But unto you that fear my name shall the Sun of righteousness arise with healing in his wings; and ye shall go forth, and grow up as calves of the stall.

The day of the Lord is the time when—the day of grace having ended—God will visit the world in judgment. Prior to that day of wrath, the first great event that will startle the world will be the disappearance of millions of people who have known and loved the Lord Jesus Christ. One moment they will be on the earth: some will be sleeping; some will be suffering in hospitals; some will be enduring pain, grief, and distress; some will be gathered together for worship. But the next moment "in the twinkling of an eye" these redeemed ones will be changed and they will disappear (1 Corinthians 15:52). The world will waken to find them gone.

I read of a gentleman who once a month went to a certain city where great steel mills were constantly pounding, pounding, pounding. He wondered how the citizens of that city could sleep, but they were so used to the noise that it did not bother them. He could get no sleep when he spent the night in that town. Then in the middle of one night, something happened to the electricity and in a moment the mills stopped. Suddenly the whole town woke up. They were so used to the noise that it put them to sleep.

The world has heard the gospel down through the centuries and still sleeps on. But some day the church will be gone and the gospel, as now preached, will be silenced. Then the world will wake up to find that it is entering the day of the Lord. "When they shall say, Peace and safety; then sudden destruction cometh upon them, as travail upon a woman with child; and they shall not escape" (1 Thessalonians 5:3).

In 1 Thessalonians 5:4 the apostle Paul turned his attention to comforting believers. The coming of the Lord will not be "as a thief in the night" for those who are waiting expectantly for His return. Those of us who are saved are "children of the day: we are not of the night, nor of darkness" (5:5). We used to be children of darkness, but God has brought us out of darkness into light.

While the world sleeps, we should be alert, awake, ever seeking to serve the Lord Jesus. We should be making His truth known to other people and we should be trying to get them ready to welcome Him when He returns. Oh, that Christians everywhere might be awakened out of their lethargy and out of their carelessness and frivolity! Oh, that they might realize the seriousness of the times in which we live! It is a solemn thing to be a Christian in a world like ours, for we will soon have to give an account of our works to the great Judge.

Those of us who are "children of light" should put on "the breast-plate of faith and love" (5:8). Faith and love will protect our hearts. As the world is drifting on to its time of great trouble, we will be garrisoned by our confidence in God.

In addition to the breastplate, Paul told us to put on "for an hel-met, the hope of salvation. For God hath not appointed us to wrath" (5:8-9). In other words, we will not be here to share in that day of wrath. We will be delivered out of this world, for we have been appointed "to obtain salvation." Here Paul had in mind our final salvation.

The world is drifting on to the day when the wrath of God will be poured out from Heaven, and Satan will be cast down to earth. The devil will then set his wrath in opposition to the wrath of God. The hour of judgment will strike, but we will be saved from it by our Lord Jesus Christ. We will be taken away in accordance with the promise to the church of Philadelphia: "Because thou hast kept the word of my patience, I also will keep thee from the hour of tempta-tion, which shall come upon all the world, to try them that dwell upon the earth" (Revelation 3:10).

As Christians we do not dwell permanently on the earth; our citi-zenship is in Heaven from whence we look for the Savior who is coming to snatch us away from the wrath to come. Some of us who are living now may still be alive when the Lord comes to catch up His saints. But whether we live until He returns or die before He comes, we know that we will all be caught up to "live together with him" (1 Thessalonians 5:10).

The apostle concluded his message about the day of the Lord by saying, "Wherefore comfort yourselves together" (5:11). There is no comfort in this message for those who are not yet saved. The day of judgment looms for those who have not come to Christ. "Now is the day of salvation" (2 Corinthians 6:2) and while the gospel is preached, God wants all to believe and live, but if men persistently reject His Son, only judgment awaits them. It is their own fault if they are left behind on the day of the rapture because God has made a way of escape, and they have failed to use it.

For those of us who are saved and who are expecting and waiting for the Lord's return, it is comforting to know that we will have no part in the woes of this world during the great tribulation. We will be with the Lord in the Father's house. When He descends to the earth to set up His kingdom, we will come with Him and reign with Him. He will appoint His redeemed ones to places of authority over this lower universe. In 1 Corinthians 6:2-3 Paul asked, "Do ye not know that the saints shall judge the world? and if the world shall be judged by you, are ye unworthy to judge the smallest matters? Know ye not that we shall judge angels?"

So we should be looking expectantly not for the day of Jehovah, but for the coming of the Lord Jesus to take us to be with Him and to be like Him forever. Hebrews 9:27-28 reassures us that "as it is appointed unto men once to die, but after this the judgment: So Christ was once offered to bear the sins of many; and unto them that look for him shall he appear the second time without sin unto salvation."

> We're watching for Jesus who entered within
> The Holiest of all when He put away sin:
> A place in the glory He's gone to prepare,
> Where we shall be with Him; but will you be there?

Exhortations (1 Thessalonians 5:12-22)

This section of the chapter consists largely of exhortations based on truth revealed already.

The admonition in verses 12-13 deals with the attitude of members of the body of Christ toward those whom God has set in their midst as spiritual guides. It is God who calls men to be His servants and entrusts them with gifts such as teaching, preaching, and administration. It is He who gives these servants to His people in order to build them up and lead them on in Christ. True pastors are spiritual shepherds who are responsible for caring for the sheep and lambs of Christ's flock. Such leaders are to be reverenced as they seek to fulfill their ministries. We are not admonished simply to approve their personalities; we are told to recognize that God has entrusted to them the ministries of teaching, preaching, and exhorting the saints.

The thought added to the end of verse 13 is an exhortation that we as Christians always need to remember: "Be at peace among yourselves." It is so easy to allow little things to set us against one another and thus bring in a spirit of strife among God's people. Whenever we realize that our hearts are contentious, we should go immediately to the Lord in humiliation and self-judgment and seek the grace not to say or do anything willfully that is likely to cause quarreling among God's children.

There are twelve distinct exhortations in 1 Thessalonians 5:14-22. They are so plain and clear that one does not need to use many words in an attempt to explain them; they are self-explanatory.

1. "Warn them that are unruly" (5:14). Some of the people found in local churches or assemblies of saints are naturally rebellious. They always want to run things to suit themselves. They have splendid dispositions as long as they can have everything their own way, but if anyone crosses them, the old nature soon shows itself. Such people are to be warned because they are hindrances to blessing.

2. "Comfort the feebleminded [faint-hearted]." Not everyone is courageous and quick to act. We must be considerate of those who are lacking in confidence and boldness.

3. "Support the weak." Instead of censuring the weak, we should assist them and put up with their infirmities. We are inclined to condemn those who are not as strong in faith as we imagine ourselves to be. But a condemning attitude is not the spirit of Christ.

4. "Be patient toward all men." Even in Christian circles, many things that try our patience might arouse ill-temper, but we are called to be considerate on all occasions.

5. "See that none render evil for evil unto any man; but ever follow that which is good, both among yourselves, and to all men" (5:15). The Christian is not to retaliate. Savonarola said, "A Christian's life consists in doing good and suffering evil." The Lord taught us what our attitude should be when we encounter evil: "Unto him that smiteth thee on the one cheek offer also the other; and him that taketh away thy cloke forbid not to take thy coat also" (Luke 6:29). The apostle Paul said elsewhere, "Recompense to no man evil for evil" (Romans 12:17). We are to return good for evil.

6. "Rejoice evermore" (1 Thessalonians 5:16). He who knows Christ can rejoice even in the midst of sorrow. Ezra said, "The joy of the Lord is your strength" (Nehemiah 8:10). If His joy disappears, we can be sure that something is wrong; something needs to be put right. George Muller, that great nineteenth-century apostle of faith, said, "I never allow myself to begin the day without facing before God anything that has left me unhappy or distressed, because I want to be before Him always in the spirit of joyfulness." We may blame others for our lack of joy, but the truth of the matter is that if our joy has gone, we have no one to blame but ourselves. It shows that we are out of fellowship with God. Our blessed Lord set the example; in spite of the fact that He was rejected by men, His spirit was always one of joyfulness and gladness as He communed with His Father.

7. "Pray without ceasing" (1 Thessalonians 5:17). We cannot always be uttering words of prayer, but we can be in the attitude of prayer continuously; that is, we can always be in the spirit of dependence on God. As hymnist James Montgomery wrote, "Prayer is the soul's sincere desire, / Uttered or unexpressed." We are to go through life with our hearts looking up to God no matter how much we may be occupied with other matters.

8. "In every thing give thanks: for this is the will of God in Christ Jesus concerning you" (5:18). Thankfulness and holiness go together. It was when men began to be unthankful that they turned away from God and went into idolatry. We can give thanks "in every thing" because "we know that all things work together for good to them that love God, to them who are the called according to his purpose"

(Romans 8:28). Giving thanks should do away with complaining. We have all seen people at the dinner table give thanks for the food God has provided, then begin to complain about it before their eyes are hardly open. To vast numbers of poverty-stricken people, that same food would seem most delicious and even sumptuous.

To give thanks "in every thing" is to recognize that all our circumstances come from God. You may ask, "Is it not Satan who brings evil things into my life?" The answer is yes, it was Satan who was permitted to afflict Job. But Job looked beyond Satan to the One who had allowed the enemy that liberty. Job said, "The Lord gave, and the Lord hath taken away; blessed be the name of the Lord....shall we receive good at the hand of God, and shall we not receive evil?" (Job 1:21; 2:10). If we remember that it is the Lord who permits the unpleasant things for our good, then we should be enabled to thank Him for them all. I should seek to learn the lessons He has for me in them.

9. "Quench not the Spirit" (1 Thessalonians 5:19). The unsaved may resist the Spirit, but it is only believers who quench the Spirit. We may also grieve that divine personality who dwells within our hearts. To quench the Spirit is to fail to respond to His guidance.

10. "Despise not prophesyings" (5:20). We are to be ready to recognize the messages of God when His servants speak. In 1 Corinthians 14:3 we read, "He that prophesieth speaketh unto men to edification, and exhortation, and comfort." A person who prophesies is not necessarily a foreteller. He may be a "forthteller," one who tells forth the mind of God; and of course his message will always be based on the Word of God.

11. "Prove all things; hold fast that which is good" (1 Thessalonians 5:21). We are to evaluate the different teachings we hear by comparing them to the Word of God, which is the only accurate test. We are to accept that which agrees with the Scriptures and reject everything else.

12. "Abstain from all appearance of evil" (5:22). We Christians are prone to forget this exhortation because of the independence of our spirits. If you for example have a habit that some think is evil, you may say that they have no right to judge you since you are not harming anyone. But you need to consider the weaker person. All

of us should remember that others are watching us and taking note of how we behave. We ought to abstain from all that looks like evil, or if we translate Paul's words literally, "from every form of evil."

Sanctification (1 Thessalonians 5:23-24)

Verse 23 has troubled many people. Some have taken for granted that sanctification means the absolute eradication of all inbred sin. But there is not one passage of Scripture that treats sanctification from that standpoint. *To sanctify* means "to set apart, to separate from that which is evil." A Christian is to be separated from worldly things, from all that is unholy (see 1 Thessalonians 4:3).

Sanctification is presented in three different ways in Scripture. First, sanctification is presented as a work that begins before we ever come to a definite knowledge of salvation. We read in 1 Peter 1:2 that we are "elect according to the foreknowledge of God the Father, through sanctification of the Spirit, unto obedience and sprinkling of the blood of Jesus Christ." In 2 Thessalonians 2:13 we read, "But we are bound to give thanks alway to God for you, brethren beloved of the Lord, because God hath from the beginning chosen you to salvation through sanctification of the Spirit and belief of the truth." Election was God's purpose in the past and this is carried out in the present by sanctification of the Spirit. The Spirit of God working within us showed us our need of a Savior and led us to trust in Christ. Then the Spirit came to dwell within us and He continues the work of sanctification all through our Christian lives. Every believer is sanctified by the Holy Spirit.

Second, sanctification is presented as positional. It is absolutely complete from the moment we believe. We are then set apart for God by virtue of the precious blood of Christ. Positional sanctification is perfect: "By one offering he hath perfected for ever them that are sanctified" (Hebrews 10:14). Nothing can ever be taken from this sanctification; nothing can be added to it. Christ Himself is our sanctification and we are complete in Him.

Third, sanctification is presented in its practical aspect. As we read and study the Word of God, wonderful truths are opened up to us; we learn from that Word what is in accordance with His will and as we obey the Word, we are practically sanctified. Jesus prayed, "Sanctify them through thy truth: thy word is truth" (John 17:17). This sanctification by the Word will not be complete until we reach the end of our pilgrimage. We are sanctified in Christ Jesus the moment we believe in Him, but as we feed on the Word and apply it to our lives, we are being sanctified by the truth.

When people tell me that they are already sanctified completely, I ask them, "Have you ever read through your Bible?" Some of them say, "No, I am afraid I cannot say that I have read it through all the way, but I have read a good deal of it." Then I reply, "Since sanctification is by the Word, how can you be sanctified completely if you have never read through your Bible?"

Our sanctification will be complete at "the coming of our Lord Jesus Christ." Then we will be wholly sanctified. "We know that, when he shall appear, we shall be like him; for we shall see him as he is" (1 John 3:2). The believer's entire spirit (the highest part of man), soul (his emotional nature), and body (then glorified) will be sanctified completely on that day and he will be altogether conformed to the Lord Jesus Christ.

Do you know Him now as your personal Savior? Do you yearn for the day when you will be absolutely free from grief, pain, and sins? Do you long to become like Him? God has called you for that purpose and He guarantees that He will bring you to that desired end in Christ Jesus. This is the precious promise of 1 Thessalonians 5:24: "Faithful is he that calleth you, who also will do it." Philippians 1:6 confirms the promise: "He which hath begun a good work in you will perform it until the day of Jesus Christ." His faithfulness is infinite.

Conclusion (1 Thessalonians 5:25-28)

Paul asked for prayer for himself and his companions as servants of Christ, missionaries of the cross, teachers of the Word of God. Those who stand in places of public testimony need the prayers of God's people. Because such teachers are so likely to fail in some way, they need prayer so that they will be able to maintain a consistent testimony for the glory of Christ as they seek to minister the Word of God.

Paul continued, "Greet all the brethren with an holy kiss" (1 Thessalonians 5:26). In his day the kiss was the customary greeting, so the emphasis here is not on the word "kiss" but on the word "holy." If our custom is to greet one another with a handshake, it should be a holy handshake. We all have seen unholy handshakes. For instance two men are talking unkindly about a third man when suddenly the third man appears; one of the two grasps the third man's hand and says, "Oh, dear brother, I am so glad to see you!" Or two women are criticizing a third woman who unexpectedly appears; one of the two runs up to her and gives her a hearty kiss. That is a "Judas kiss." If your attitude toward others is holy, you will never be embarrassed by the sudden appearance of a "third" person. The apostle was stressing the importance of reality in our greetings.

Before concluding his letter, Paul gave one more instruction to the Thessalonians: "I charge you by the Lord that this epistle be read unto all the holy brethren" (5:27). Notice the expression "holy brethren." The apostle dared to use that term because in Christ all believers are holy before God.

The Epistle closes with the usual Pauline benediction: "The grace of our Lord Jesus Christ be with you. Amen." (5:28).

SECOND
THESSALONIANS

CHAPTER ONE
DIVINE
RETRIBUTION

P aul's first Epistle to the Thessalonians dealt largely with the coming of the Lord Jesus Christ for His saints. Evidently some Christians in Thessalonica misunderstood the teaching in that letter. They seem to have jumped to the conclusion that since the Lord's coming might take place at any moment, it was useless for them to work for a living. And since they were going through some very trying and distressing experiences, they thought that perhaps they were already entering the great tribulation. The apostle, who was still in Corinth, heard of these strange misunderstandings of the truth that he had sought to explain and wrote a second letter in order to correct these unwholesome views. He wanted to explain more definitely and clearly what the responsibilities of Christians are as they wait for the coming of the Lord Jesus Christ.

Apostolic Salutation (2 Thessalonians 1:1-2)

"Paul, and Silvanus, and Timotheus, unto the church of the Thessalonians in God our Father and the Lord Jesus Christ" (1:1). The salutation here is the same as the salutation in 1 Thessalonians. It is only in these two letters that we find a local church spoken of as "the church...in God our Father and the Lord Jesus Christ." The emphasis is on family relationship: the Christians in Thessalonica were young believers, but they knew God as Father. They were children in His family and Jesus Christ was their Lord.

The apostle wished them grace and peace. They would need grace for every step of the way and as they learned to trust in the living

Father, they would enjoy the peace of God. His peace would protect their hearts and give them quiet confidence as they pursued the pilgrim journey through this troubled world.

Comfort for the Persecuted (2 Thessalonians 1:3-10)

In this passage the apostle sought to comfort and encourage these believers who were enduring great suffering and persecution for Christ's sake. To console and hearten the saints amidst their trials and perplexities, Paul wrote, "We are bound to thank God always for you, brethren, as it is meet, because that your faith groweth exceedingly, and the charity of every one of you all toward each other aboundeth" (1:3). The English word "love" is a better rendering, I think, than the older word "charity" because over the years the thought of almsgiving has been attached to the word "charity." Paul was speaking here of sincere affection, not of kind consideration for others—although real love is always charitable.

Paul gave the church at Thessalonica credit for two things: a growing faith and abounding love. It is a wonderful thing when Christians are characterized in this way. Too often believers who have been Christians for many years look back to the old days and ask:

> Where is the blessedness I knew
> When first I saw the Lord?
> Where is that soul-refreshing view
> Of Jesus and His Word?
>   (William Cowper)

They think of early joys as they sing:

> O happy day that fixed my choice
> On Thee, my Savior and my God!

But they are not able to finish the verse, for it does not describe their present condition:

> Well may this glowing heart rejoice
> And tell its raptures all abroad.
>   (Philip Doddridge)

It is a pitiable thing when a Christian's present state is lower than it was when he was first converted. This was true of the believers at Ephesus when the Lord had to say to the church there, "I have somewhat against thee, because thou hast left thy first love" (Revelation 2:4). But it was otherwise with the Thessalonian believers. Some time had elapsed since they were converted, but their faith was growing and they were abounding in love.

Perhaps we need to search our own hearts and ask ourselves some questions: Is our faith growing "exceedingly"? Do we have more confidence in God today than we had when we came to Him in the beginning of our Christian lives? Have we proved and tested Him through the years so that we know we can count on Him now in a larger and fuller way than we did when we were first brought to know Him? If we cannot answer yes, it is evident that we are in a backslidden condition. Our faith is declining and we need to turn to God and cry, "Restore unto me the joy of thy salvation" (Psalm 51:12). Proverbs 4:18 tells us that "the path of the just is as the shining light, that shineth more and more unto the perfect day," so we who have known the Lord for years ought to be stronger in faith than ever before. Our love should be abounding more and more each passing day.

The Thessalonian believers were passing through a time of great suffering, tribulation, and bitter anguish for Christ's sake, but the grace of God was wonderfully evident in their lives. Their enemies could not understand how they could be so joyous and peaceful in spite of the persecutions that they were enduring. Unbelievers, who wondered how these Christians could continue in holy, happy unity, surely said, "How is it that they do not seem to be moved by our efforts to upset them? They go right on rejoicing, returning love for hatred, kindness for malice, and praying for those who persecute them. We do not understand." Such behavior should always be characteristic of those who are redeemed by the Lord Jesus Christ.

We are made heirs of the kingdom by the new birth, but we prove that we are "worthy of the kingdom of God" by readily enduring suffering for Christ's sake (2 Thessalonians 1:5). We are told that if we suffer with Him, we will also reign with Him (2 Timothy 2:12). All believers suffer with Him in some sense, but all do not suffer for Him in the same way. One could not be a Christian at all—could not be indwelt by the Holy Spirit—if he did not suffer with Christ. The very fact that we belong to Him and have received a new and divine nature makes us suffer as we go through this world that has rejected Him. But Paul had something more than that in mind in 2 Thessalonians 1:5. He was referring to taking so definite a stand for Christ that we become the objects of the world's hatred. If we are prepared to endure grief and wrong because of our faithfulness to Christ, we will have the opportunity to prove ourselves worthy of that kingdom to which we are heirs.

The apostle went on to assure the suffering Thessalonians that God would rightfully "recompense tribulation to them that trouble you" (1:6). We are to love our enemies, bless them that curse us, and pray for them that despitefully use us, but in His own time God will deal with those who have persecuted His church.

When the Lord Jesus Christ comes in judgment, a great distinction will be made between those who knew and loved the Savior and those who, refusing to believe the gospel, persisted in their sins and wickedness in utter indifference to the God who created them. Those who have persecuted the church and are still alive will receive retribution at that second coming (those who have already died will be judged at the last great assize). But Christ will take care of His persecuted people when He descends "to recompense tribulation." Paul told the Thessalonians that God would recompense rest to those the wicked have sought to injure (1:7). "When the Lord Jesus shall be revealed from heaven with his mighty angels," He will repay trouble and anguish to those who deserve His wrath, but He will reward all who are His own with rest, joy, and comfort.

Second Thessalonians 1:7-8 refers not to the coming of the Lord for His own (as in 1 Thessalonians 4) but to the day of the Lord (as in 1 Thessalonians 5). Revelation 1:7 also refers to the day of the Lord when it says, "Behold, he cometh with clouds; and every eye shall see him, and they also which pierced him: and all kindreds of the earth shall wail because of him." On that day He will come as Judge to destroy those who have spurned His grace. This second coming will usher in that glorious era when the Lord Jesus will reign in righteousness over the whole earth.

On the day of the Lord, He will be revealed "in flaming fire taking vengeance on them that know not God, and that obey not the gospel" (2 Thessalonians 1:8). Here Paul referred to two classes of people. In the first class are those who "know not God"; these are the heathen who have lived in ignorance of the gospel and in definite rebellion against their Creator. In the second class are those who "obey not the gospel"; that is, they have heard the truth, but have rejected it.

People ask, "Is God going to judge the heathen? Is He going to send them to Hell for rejecting Jesus Christ when they never heard of Him?" The answer is no. He is not going to send them to Hell for rejecting Jesus Christ, but He is going to judge them for their sins. We read in Romans 1 that they have been given up to uncleanness because they have sinned against their own consciences and against the God they once knew. So whether or not the Word has ever been taken to them by missionaries, they are sinning against the light that God has given them.

The guiltier class are those who "obey not the gospel of our Lord Jesus Christ." Men and women who live in this favored land should consider this fact with intense solemnity. When I hear people talking glibly about the heathen and what God will do with them, I feel that it would be far better for them to be thinking about themselves. What will God do with those who have heard the message over and over again and have spurned it? What will He do with those who have known of Christ all their lives and have rejected His love and grace?

One of the saddest things I know is to see young men and women living careless, indifferent lives after growing up in Christian homes. They have had examples of piety in godly fathers or mothers and the benefits of being raised where family worship was maintained, yet they leave their childhood homes saying that they had enough religion when they were young and do not want it now. How such stupid expressions reveal the rebellion of the heart and hardness of conscience! For these rebellious individuals there is nothing but judgment unless they repent, break down before God, confess their sins, and turn to the Christ whom they have rejected.

When the Lord Jesus comes in the clouds "in flaming fire," He will punish those who have sinned with no knowledge of Christ; but with more intense wrath he will punish those who have sinned against the light and knowledge that God has given them concerning His beloved Son. The latter, we read, "shall be punished with everlasting destruction from the presence of the Lord, and from the glory of his power" (2 Thessalonians 1:9). What solemn words! What terrible warnings God has given men in order that they might face the question of their guilt and turn to Him in repentance! Like the danger signals at railroad crossings, He is saying, "Stop! Look! Listen!"

How sad it would be to be found in one's sin "when he shall come to be glorified in his saints, and to be admired in all them that believe" (1:10). What a great separation there will be "in that day." Gathered about Christ will be those who believed the message, trusted Him as Savior, and maintained a testimony for Him on earth, but were misunderstood and persecuted for His name's sake; these will rejoice with Him in the day of His power. On the other hand, those who spurned His lovingkindness will experience the awfulness of divine retribution.

Paul's Prayer (2 Thessalonians 1:11-12)

The chapter closes with the apostle's prayer for the saints: "Wherefore also we pray always for you, that our God would count you worthy of this calling, and fulfill all the good pleasure of his goodness, and the work of faith with power" (1:11). We would do well to use the same expressions and pray for grace to act accordingly—grace to walk "worthy of this calling." It is a privilege to be allowed to walk with the Lord through a world that rejects Him; it is a privilege to bear His name when that name is despised by the godless. How many of us look upon it as a privilege?

Paul ended his prayer with these words: "That the name of our

Lord Jesus Christ may be glorified in you, and ye in Him, according to the grace of our God and the Lord Jesus Christ" (1:12). As our love abounds there will be increased power in our lives to witness for Christ and to glorify Him.

The Christian walks a path of rejection as he goes through the world, but ahead of him is the glorious prospect of joy with Christ at His return. Ahead of the unsaved is nothing but judgment in that day when "the Lord Jesus shall be revealed from heaven...in flaming fire taking vengeance on them that know not God, and that obey not the gospel."

CHAPTER TWO
EVERLASTING CONSOLATION

The Rise of the Antichrist (2 Thessalonians 2:1-12)

As we begin to consider the special line of truth that is the subject of this passage, we need to remind ourselves that the outstanding theme of the first Epistle to the Thessalonians is the coming of the Lord Jesus Christ to receive His own *before* the onset of the awful period of judgment that is designated in the Old Testament as the day of the Lord, a time of trouble, or the time of Jacob's trouble. Our Lord Jesus spoke of the period as the great tribulation.

The Thessalonian believers were looking forward to the appearing of the Lord. They were waiting for Him to return to earth to execute judgment on the wicked and set up His kingdom in this place where He had been rejected and crucified. It was this aspect of His coming that had made the deepest impression on their hearts even though Paul had explained that the Lord will first come in the air for His saints.

Sometimes believers have very poor memories and these Thessalonians seemed to have forgotten this truth, which Paul had endeavored to make so clear in his first letter. So when they encountered bitter persecution and trouble, they began to wonder if the day of the Lord had begun; they thought they might already be in the midst of the great tribulation. They completely lost sight of the truth that had been revealed concerning the rapture of the church.

It seems that someone had misled them into believing that they were experiencing the throes of the time of Jehovah's wrath. Presumably this person had asserted that he had been given a special revelation from God, and many of the brethren had been deceived.

It seems too that someone had forged a letter in the name of the apostle Paul in which he definitely declared that the day of the Lord really had begun and the church was going through the great tribulation.

In order to correct these false beliefs, the apostle wrote his second Epistle to the Thessalonians. In the first chapter of his second letter he declared the truth concerning the Lord's judgment that will take place when He is "revealed from heaven with his mighty angels, In flaming fire taking vengeance on them that know not God, and that obey not the gospel of our Lord Jesus Christ" (2 Thessalonians 1:7-8). Before this time of vengeance, believers of this church age will have been caught up in the clouds "to meet the Lord in the air" (1 Thessalonians 4:17), but they will appear with Him in great glory when He descends as depicted in 2 Thessalonians 1.

In 2 Thessalonians 2:1-12 the apostle emphasized the fact that the day of the Lord cannot begin while the church is still on the earth. He wanted his readers to remember that the hope of believers is that they will be gathered together unto the Lord before judgment falls upon the earth. They were not to give heed to the theory that they were entering the great tribulation era—even though someone had professed to have discovered such teaching in the Word, or to have spoken by the Spirit, or to have received a letter from Paul asserting the theory.

In 2 Thessalonians 2:2 Paul cautioned his readers not to believe "that the day of Christ is at hand" (King James version). Here "the day of Christ" is a faulty translation. The best manuscript authority renders the original as "the day of the Lord." The two phrases refer to two very different events. The day of Christ is the time when believers receive their rewards at the judgment seat of Christ immediately after the rapture. The day of the Lord, as we have seen, is the period when Jehovah's judgments will be poured out, culminating in the literal return of the Lord Jesus to this world, where He will set up the kingdom of God.

The day of Christ is always imminent. There are no signs to be looked for; the Son may return from Heaven at any time. It is not to this precious and glorious event that 2 Thessalonians 2:2 refers, but to the next stage of Christ's second advent and the judgments immediately preceding it.

Almost invariably when the church is called on to go through a time of great suffering, there are those who jump to the conclusion that it must be the beginning of "the hour of temptation, which shall come upon all the world to try them that dwell upon the earth" (Revelation 3:10). In our own generation we have passed through two world wars; in each of these awful conflicts, a large part of the professing church of Christ endured great suffering, and many teachers began to assert that we were entering the great tribulation.

Some have taught that the church must go through the entire tribulation period which, according to the book of Daniel, is to take place in the last and unfulfilled seventieth week of the great prophecy of chapter 9. This seven-week period is all a time of tribulation, but it is divided in Scripture into two parts: the first three-and-one-half years is a time of preliminary and largely providential judgment; the last three-and-one-half years cover the great tribulation proper when the wrath of the Lamb and the wrath of God will be poured out on the world, and Satan will be cast down from the heavens.

Some who realize that the church is to be saved from the wrath, and therefore cannot agree with the idea that it will go through the entire seven-week period of judgment, have taught that the church will go through at least the first half of the week. If this teaching were true, two companies of saints would be on earth at the same time: the heavenly company (the church, which is the body of Christ) and the earthly company (the remnant of Israel, who are to be gathered out of the apostate nation at the beginning of the tribulation).

To conclude that both companies will be on earth at the same time is unthinkable if one considers the Scriptures relating to each company. God has both a heavenly and an earthly election. In our Lord's great prophetic discourse recorded in Matthew 24, the elect to be gathered out of all nations when He descends to set up His kingdom are Israel and those Gentiles who, having "washed their robes, and made them white in the blood of the Lamb" (Revelation 7:14), will come out of great tribulation. The elect of the Epistles are a heavenly company, the "church of the firstborn" whose names are written in Heaven (Hebrews 12:23).

As Christians we ought to realize that ours is indeed a heavenly hope. We are not to be occupied with events and conditions down here; we should be looking for our blessed Lord to snatch us away from the wrath to come. The day of the Lord cannot begin until after this has taken place.

Paul said, "That day shall not come, except there come a falling away first, and that man of sin be revealed, the son of perdition" (2 Thessalonians 2:3). The "man of sin" is undoubtedly the same as the personal antichrist of whom the apostle John spoke in his Epistles and the king who "shall do according to his own will" in Daniel's great prophecy. The day of the Lord cannot come until the "man of sin" has been revealed and he will not be revealed prior to the rapture. We therefore are never instructed to look for the rising up of this sinister personage who occupies such a large place in prophecies that relate to the last days.

After the church has been caught up, the apostasy of Christendom and Judaism will be complete. Among the vast throng of people left on earth will be many who, though unconverted, have professed faith; these will throw off all pretension of allegiance to Christ and to God. That complete "falling away," or apostasy, will be the preparation for the reception of the antichrist. When the Jews are gathered back to their own land in unbelief, these words of the Lord Jesus will be fulfilled: "I am come in my Father's name, and ye receive me not: if another shall come in his own name, him ye will receive" (John 5:43). The one who will "come in his own name" is the "man of sin...the son of perdition."

The "man of sin" will proclaim himself to be the incarnation of God; he will exalt himself "above all that is called God, or that is worshipped" (2 Thessalonians 2:4). This antichrist will sit in the temple that the returning Jews will build in the land of Palestine and to him will be rendered the worship that belongs to God alone. As Daniel prophesied in 11:36-37:

> The king shall do according to his will; and he shall exalt himself, and magnify himself above every god, and shall speak

marvellous things against the God of gods, and shall prosper till
the indignation be accomplished: for that that is determined
shall be done. Neither shall he regard the God of his fathers, nor
the desire of women, nor regard any god: for he shall magnify
himself above all.

We know that this mysterious king will be a Jew because he is
said not to "regard the God of his fathers." In Scripture "the God of
his fathers" refers invariably to the God of Abraham, the God of
Isaac, and the God of Jacob. "The desire of women" undoubtedly
refers to the Messiah, since every Jewish woman hoped to be the
mother of the Deliverer of Israel. So the "man of sin" will be the
son of Jewish parents and he will present himself to Israel as God
manifest in the flesh, the Messiah for whom they have waited.

It is evident that Paul had taught his readers about the antichrist
when he was in Thessalonica, for he said, "Remember ye not, that,
when I was yet with you, I told you these things?" (2 Thessalonians
2:5) Of course in the short time that he was in that city he could not
have made everything clear, and even if he had, much would have
been forgotten. So when circumstances arose that filled the
Thessalonians with fear and dread, they became so focused on these
conditions that they lost the hope of the return of Christ to take His
people away before the judgments begin.

In 2 Thessalonians 2:6-7 the apostle explained something that
every believer ought to understand and many students and teachers
of prophecy have misunderstood: "Ye know what withholdeth that
he [the antichrist] might be revealed in his time. For the mystery of
iniquity doth already work: only he who now letteth will let, until
he be taken out of the way." Some of the words in these verses have
changed their meaning in the course of the centuries. For example
when the King James version of the Bible was published, the word
"let" meant "hinder"; now it means "permit." What the apostle was
really saying in these verses is this: "Ye know what restraineth that
he might be revealed in his own time. For the mystery of lawless-
ness doth already work: only there is One who now hindereth, until
He be taken out of the way."

Observe that Paul suggested that his readers should know what "hindereth." Some have supposed that the apostle was referring to the Roman empire, whose downfall he had told the Thessalonians privately would take place before the second coming of Christ. It has been said that he spoke in a cryptic way because if he had spoken more clearly, he would have endangered both himself and other Christians and subjected them to the suspicions of the ruling powers.

Others have thought that Paul was referring to orderly government. In other words, a state of anarchy must prevail throughout the world before the antichrist is revealed and the Lord returns from Heaven.

But all such speculation seems needless in view of the fact that Paul was writing not merely for the Thessalonians or other believers living at that time, but also for future generations of Christians; his words would be read until the end of the dispensation. He spoke to us all when he said, "Ye know what restraineth."

My reader, if you are a Christian, you ought to know what restrains the full demonstration of evil. Do you know? I have asked Christian audiences this question many times, and they have never failed to answer correctly. Yes, it is the Holy Spirit who restrains. Isaiah 59:19 tells us, "When the enemy shall come in like a flood, the Spirit of the Lord shall lift up a standard against him." This verse has also been translated, "The Spirit of the Lord shall restrain him."

The Holy Spirit is in the world, where He is working in and through the church of God. He indwells every believer individually and the church collectively; therefore as long as the church is in the world, the antichrist will not be revealed.

Of course as 1 John 2:18 tells us, "Even now are there many antichrists." Everyone who denies the Father and the Son is an antichrist. But we are speaking here of the "man of sin," "the son of perdition," the one who will "come in his own name," the archdeceiver who will appear at the end of the age. This antichrist will not be revealed as long as the Spirit of God is in the world.

The Holy Spirit came to abide with the church forever, so as long as the church is here, He will be here. But when the church is caught up to be with the Lord, the Spirit of God will no longer be in the world in the sense in which He has been here during the Christian era.

We sometimes sing, "The Holy Ghost is leading / Home to the Lamb His Bride." Like Abraham's servant, the Spirit of God has come down to this far country to find a bride for the Son. It is the Holy Spirit who works in the hearts of men and women, leading them to Christ. When His work is completed, He will go up with the church "and then shall that Wicked be revealed" (2 Thessalonians 2:8).

This lawless one, who will set himself up as God incarnate, will be the special object of divine judgment; he will be destroyed by the Lord Himself when He returns in power and glory. We learn from Revelation 19:20 that he will be cast alive into the lake of fire.

During his brief time of power on earth the antichrist will deceive the nations with all kinds of false miracles and "lying wonders" (2 Thessalonians 2:9). Jesus said that if it were possible, the very elect would be deceived by him (Matthew 24:24). But, thank God, it is not possible, "for they know not the voice of strangers" (John 10:5); they will hear the voice of the Good Shepherd. The propaganda of the antichrist will carry away those who "received not the love of the truth, that they might be saved" (2 Thessalonians 2:10). In fact it is God Himself who in righteous judgment will give them up to be deluded. We read in 2:11, "God shall send them strong delusion, that they should believe a lie." Instead of "a lie," we might read, "*the* lie": the lie that the "man of sin" is the Christ of God.

This is a solemn word indeed for those who hear the gospel in our day and definitely reject it. If they are still rejecting the truth when the rapture of the church takes place, there will be no hope of their turning to Christ during the period of tribulation. Having believed the lie, they will be judged with all those who have apostatized from the truth.

If you have not yet received Christ, the following words are for you. No doubt many of you who are unsaved are children of Christian parents. You have heard the name of Christ all your lives, yet you have never definitely accepted Him. If Jesus should come today, you would be among the number who will receive the antichrist. You will probably say, "Impossible! I have been too well-taught for that; I have heard the gospel too many times. I have learned the great outlines of prophecy, and I know something of the divine program. I would not be deceived in that way. I would turn immediately to the Lord after He had taken His church out of the world, and thus I would be prepared to welcome Him at His glorious appearing." But according to the Word of God, that will not happen. If you reject Christ now, you will have no desire to accept Him in the coming day of tribulation. You are in the most dangerous position anyone could be in. The Word of the Lord says, "He, that being often reproved hardeneth his neck, shall suddenly be destroyed, and that without remedy" (Proverbs 29:1).

Some of the saddest funerals I have had to conduct have been for unsaved young people who were members of Christian families. These young men and women had often been urged to come to Christ, but they had gone on in carelessness, hoping that everything would come out all right in the end. Then suddenly they were struck down, perhaps by accident, and they went out into eternity leaving no testimony.

If you are unsaved, I plead with you not to allow another day to pass without coming to Christ, lest the near future find you forever beyond all hope of mercy. God has given you the opportunity to believe the truth; He has presented His Word. But if you turn away from that truth and refuse to believe the gospel, then God Himself may give you up to delusion so that you will believe the lie of the "man of sin" and so be eternally lost.

Salvation through Sanctification (2 Thessalonians 2:13-17)

Having spoken of the apostasy of the last days and the coming of the "man of sin" when the hinderer, the Holy Spirit, will no longer be working on the earth, the apostle turned to comforting the saints with the assurance that they were the special objects of divine care. His words apply to Christians everywhere, for all such are "brethren beloved of the Lord" and everyone of them has been chosen by God from the beginning for salvation "through sanctification of the Spirit and belief of the truth" (2 Thessalonians 2:13). We read in

Romans 8:29, "Whom he did foreknow, he also did predestinate to be conformed to the image of his Son." Looking down through the ages God foreknew all who would ever put their trust in the Lord Jesus Christ and He chose them to be conformed to Christ. If you are a believer in the Lord Jesus Christ, you need never worry about your election. The very fact that you are a believer, redeemed by Christ, assures you that you are among the elect of God.

Notice that God has chosen you "to *salvation* through *sanctification*" (italics added). That means we were aroused to realize our lost condition and our need of a Savior by the direct work of the Holy Spirit and thus we were led to trust in the Lord Jesus Christ. Sanctification of the Spirit is the initial work of God in the soul, and then when we believe the gospel we have the assurance of salvation.

Paul told the Romans that he was a minister of God to the nations so that "the offering up of the Gentiles might be acceptable, being sanctified by the Holy Ghost" (Romans 15:16). A man may preach the Word with great liberty and power, but unless the Holy Spirit applies the Word to the hearts, illumines the minds, and troubles the consciences of his listeners, his preaching will never convert a single person.

Those of us who are saved can look back and recall how the work of the Holy Spirit began in our souls. We remember the time when we were just part and parcel of the world around us, and then there came an awakening. Perhaps at first we could not understand what was happening to us. We became unhappy and dissatisfied; we desired something we had never known before; we became conscious of our sinfulness and guilt; and we cried out in our hearts for cleansing and purity—that was the sanctification of the Holy Spirit.

There is a beautiful illustration of this sanctification in Genesis 1:1-2. We read in the first verse, "In the beginning God created the heaven and the earth." That creation, we learn from Isaiah 45, was absolutely perfect, like everything else that comes from God's hand. But in Genesis 1:2 we read, "The earth was without form, and void." Most Hebrew scholars feel that a better rendering would be, "The earth became without form, and void." Whether or not this change from perfection to formlessness had to do with the fall of angels, we cannot be sure, but we do know that a tremendous catastrophe took place and the earth was plunged into chaos.

"And darkness was upon the face of the deep." The scene was one of gloom and desolation, but then "the Spirit of God moved upon the face of the waters." The word translated "moved" is sometimes used to describe a hen brooding over her nest, so we could say that "the Spirit of God *brooded* upon the face of the waters." A brooding hen, although she seems quiet and inert, is actually in constant motion. Every muscle is quivering and this generates the warmth needed to hatch the eggs. So we see the Holy Spirit moving—brooding—over the waste of waters in preparation for the reorganization of the earth in order to make it fit to be man's dwelling place.

That same blessed Holy Spirit broods over fallen man—that is, He does His sanctifying work in the sinner's heart—and then when the light shines in, the soul is saved. "God said, Let there be light: and there was light" (Genesis 1:3). This was the beginning of the new order. Psalm 119:130 tells us, "The entrance of thy words giveth light," but no man sees the light until he has been wakened from his sleep by the Holy Spirit.

So as 2 Thessalonians 2:13 tells us, we are chosen "to salvation through sanctification of the Spirit and belief of the truth." First Peter 1:2 says of the elect that the Spirit's sanctification leads them into the obedience of faith, which brings them to the "sprinkling of the blood of Jesus Christ." When we, like Israel on Passover night, take our place in faith beneath that sprinkled blood, we become absolutely secure, for Jehovah said, "When I see the blood, I will pass over you" (Exodus 12:13).

Another New Testament passage that mentions the Spirit's sanctification is 1 Corinthians 6:9-11. There Paul listed a number of evil characters (including some so vile and unclean that I almost feel like refraining from mentioning them) and then added, "Such were some of you: but ye are washed, but ye are sanctified, but ye are justified in the name of the Lord Jesus, and by the Spirit of our God." Some of the Corinthians had lived evil lives, but they had been washed by the application of the Word of God, sanctified by the Holy Spirit, and justified in the name of the Lord Jesus. This is the order in Scripture: The Word of God is proclaimed, heard, or read. The Spirit of God sanctifies—He convicts the sinner, bringing him to the place where he desires to be saved and is ready to receive Christ. Believing the gospel, the sinner is justified by faith.

Let me give some advice to those who seek to win souls: Do not try to rush people into confessing Christ. Do not try to make them say they are saved. Try to find out if there is any real conviction of sin. Try to find out if the Spirit of God has awakened them.

The reason a great many people make a profession of Christianity in revival meetings and soon afterward drift back into their former ways is that there has been no real work of God in their souls. They have never been sanctified by the Holy Spirit; they have never known divine conviction. First people need to be awakened to see their need of Christ; then the gospel can be given to them. That is the divine order. Sanctification by the Spirit leads to "belief of the truth."

When people believe the gospel message, they may be assured of eventually sharing the glory of our Lord Jesus Christ: "He called you by our gospel, to the obtaining of the glory of our Lord Jesus Christ" (2 Thessalonians 2:14). This is the purpose for which God is sending His gospel out into the world.

When people have been really born again, they will continue in the Christian life. We hear a great deal about backsliders, but some one has well said that many who are designated as backsliders have never been frontsliders; they have never been born again. In Philippians 1:6 we read, "He which hath begun a good work in you will perform it until the day of Jesus Christ."

The Thessalonians had listened to the apostle and had also received his written word, and in 2 Thessalonians 2:15 they were exhorted not to let anything turn them aside from the truth that had been proclaimed. "Therefore, brethren," Paul wrote, "stand fast, and hold the traditions which ye have been taught, whether by word, or our epistle." Do not misunderstand what the apostle said. He had not added human traditions to the Word of the Lord. But he had taught the Thessalonians certain truths by word of mouth and he urged them to retain these teachings as well as those he had committed to writing.

Today we no longer have inspired apostles proclaiming the Word; nothing is left for us but the written Word. We have no need of traditions, for we have the completed Scriptures. As 2 Timothy 3:16-17 tells us, "All scripture is given by inspiration of God, and is profitable for doctrine, for reproof, for correction, for instruction in righteousness: That the man of God may be perfect, throughly furnished unto all good works."

When our Lord was on earth, He told the scribes and Pharisees that they had made "the word of God of none effect" through their traditions (Mark 7:13). There are those today who have added a great many human traditions to the Word and have utterly confused their followers. But those who honor the Scriptures need no human traditions.

Drawing 2 Thessalonians 2 to a close, Paul wrote of God's gifts of "everlasting consolation and good hope" (2:16). Our consolation (comfort) will continue throughout eternity. Our hope will never be disappointed. The apostle also wrote of believers being established "in every good word and work" (2:17). We are not saved by good works or by any effort or behavior of our own. But because we have been saved "through sanctification of the Spirit and belief of the truth," we are responsible to maintain good works. Thus we adorn the gospel of Christ.

CHAPTER THREE
CHRISTIANITY IN PRACTICE

Five Themes (2 Thessalonians 3:1-5)

In these five verses the apostle sought to impress on the hearts of the young Thessalonian Christians—and every one of us—some thoughts on the following five topics.

1. *Prayerfulness.* In verse 1 the Thessalonians were asked to remember in prayer the one who wrote this letter. He was the mightiest evangelist, missionary, and teacher of the Word that the church of God has ever known, yet he felt the need of the prayers of these converts so that he could better fulfill his ministry.

How often do you pray for those who are called to preach the Word to others? When you are alone with God, do you remember to pray for Christ's undershepherds who seek to care for His flock? Do you pray for missionaries who have gone forth into the regions beyond for the Lord Jesus? Do you remember those who labor in the home fields—often in hard places where there is little to offer cheer and encouragement? Many of God's people cannot preach, or teach, or travel abroad to take the Word to distant lands; but all can pray.

People sometimes say to me, "I do not know what I should pray for. When I get down on my knees, I intend to spend some time in prayer, but in a few moments I have said everything that is on my heart and there seems to be nothing else to pray about." If this is your experience, why not wait quietly before God at such a time, and ask Him to bring to your mind those who are preaching and teaching the Word. Then as they come to mind, mention them individually to God. Pray that they may be sustained and kept from discouragement. There is no one who needs prayer more than those who are bearing the burden and heat of the day in the terrific battle for righteousness.

Paul had preached the gospel to the Thessalonians and he called on them to pray for blessing as he and his companions went elsewhere with their witness. Just as these Thessalonians prayed for Paul, believers today may cooperate with those who are engaged in public ministry. Then when we all appear before the judgment seat of Christ, and the Lord gives out rewards for faithful service, He will see to it that recognition is given not only to those who have preached the Word, but also to those who have backed up His servants in prayer.

You may not be qualified to go to the missionfield, but as you remain at home and give of your means to help support a missionary in Africa, China, South America, or a distant island, you will have a large part in his ministry. You may never stand in a pulpit to preach the Word, but by your prayers and intercessions you can bear up those who do.

I am sure of this: if we prayed more for God's messengers, we would criticize them less. Some people are constantly finding fault with servants of Christ. From the standpoint of these critics, His messengers never do exactly the right thing. If one of them speaks much about sin, he is too stern; if he says more about the comfort and consolation that is in Christ, he is too soft. If he talks especially to the unsaved, he is neglecting the saints; if he addresses himself particularly to Christians, he is neglecting evangelism. It is easy to get into a criticizing mood. But when we are bearing up God's servants in prayer, the spirit of criticism gives way to one of loving helpfulness.

2. *Preservation.* Since the apostle and his companions were exposed to great dangers, he said, "Pray for us...that we may be delivered from unreasonable and wicked men: for all men have not faith" (2 Thessalonians 3:1-2).

It is a sad fact that some men will never believe, no matter how clearly and tenderly the gospel is preached. Many do not have faith because they have closed their hearts and minds to the Word of God. Some say, "I have heard the gospel message over and over and I cannot believe the Bible; I cannot believe in the virgin birth of Christ; I cannot believe that He was the Son of God; I cannot believe in His physical resurrection from the dead; I cannot believe in His ascension to Heaven; I cannot believe that He is coming again." I can tell you why they cannot believe. They cannot believe because they have no desire to be free from their sins. They roll sin as a sweet morsel under their tongues, and as long as their sin means more to them than a place in Heaven, they will never be able to believe. Such are the people the apostle described as "unreasonable and wicked men."

God's gospel is reasonable. He says, "Come now, and let us reason together, saith the Lord: though your sins be as scarlet, they shall be as white as snow; though they be red like crimson, they shall be as wool" (Isaiah 1:18). He wants to reason with men; He wants them to sit down and face thoughtfully the great eternal truths that are presented in His Word. In 1 Corinthians 10:15 Paul said, "I speak as to wise men; judge ye what I say." The apostle wanted the Corinthians to exercise reason as they considered what he had said; he wanted them to think it through.

Some people will never ponder the truths of Scripture because they are determined not to believe. They do not wish to be delivered from their evil habits; therefore they are unreasonable and they reject the gospel. Unreasonableness itself is wickedness. God says, "Let the wicked forsake his way, and the unrighteous man his thoughts: and let him return unto the Lord, and he will have mercy upon him; and to our God, for he will abundantly pardon" (Isaiah 55:7). But if men have no desire to turn from their sins and be delivered from their unrighteousness, He will not force them to do so. God commands all men to repent and if they refuse, He must deal with them in judgment.

"Unreasonable and wicked men ...have not faith." Some people have been troubled by these words, which have been misinterpreted as meaning that God does not give faith to everyone and therefore some individuals cannot believe.

Scripture says, "By grace are ye saved through faith; and that not of yourselves: it is the gift of God" (Ephesians 2:8). In other words, the very faith by which we are saved is a gift of God. One view is that if the gift is not given by God to some individuals, they cannot believe and therefore should not be held responsible for the loss of their souls. But that interpretation is unsound, for Scripture also says, "Faith cometh by hearing, and hearing by the word of God" (Romans 10:17). When men give attention to the voice of God and desire to be delivered from their sins, faith springs up in their souls and they are enabled to believe in Christ and be saved. But when men deliberately spurn the Word of God and persist in their sinfulness, they are numbered among those who "have not faith." They do not have faith because they will not give heed to the message.

3. *Protection.* There is a wonderful promise in 2 Thessalonians 3:3: "The Lord is faithful, who shall stablish you, and keep you from evil." The promise is for young Christians—and old ones too— but here Paul was thinking particularly of the young believers in Thessalonica. They were very much on his heart. He knew they were exposed to all kinds of danger; he knew that Satan would do all he could to turn them away from the simplicity of the gospel of Christ. Paul had prayed for them, even as he had asked them to pray for him. He had confidence in the faithfulness of God.

God is faithful! He gives eternal life to all who believe in Him and He has promised, "They shall never perish, neither shall any man pluck them out of my hand" (John 10:28). Nothing "shall separate us from the love of Christ" (Romans 8:35). The life that the believer receives is not conditional, but eternal—therefore that life can never be lost. Those who reason otherwise show that they have never understood the meaning of salvation by pure grace. They still think of human merit as a condition for final salvation. This is the essence of Roman Catholic theology, but many Protestants have never been delivered from it.

The instructed Christian rests not on any imagined faithfulness of his own, but on the faithfulness of God, whose gifts and callings "are without repentance" (Romans 11:29). He can be depended on to establish us and to keep us from all evil as we seek to walk in obedience to his revealed will. If at times our feet slip because of self-confidence or lack of prayerfulness—like Peter in the high priest's porch—He knows how to restore our souls and bring us back to the path of obedience.

4. *Perseverance.* The apostle had confidence in the saints (see 2 Thessalonians 3:4). They had believed in Christ and Paul believed in them. Paul knew that those who had trusted Christ were saved, and he counted on seeing them come out on top. We should not get into the habit of underrating and misunderstanding God's people. I know that many of God's dear children are enthusiastic for a time and then their keen interest seems to dissipate as they drift away from their first love. But the fact that the Spirit of God dwells in them is good reason for confidence that they will be recovered; they will come at last to the path of subjection to the will of the Lord.

5. *Patience.* Oh, how much we need the patience mentioned in 2 Thessalonians 3:5! A better rendering of the verse would read, "The Lord direct your hearts into the love of God, and into the *patience* of Christ."

We see the patience of Christ illustrated in James 5:7: "Be patient therefore, brethren, unto the coming of the Lord. Behold, the husbandman waiteth for the precious fruit of the earth, and hath long patience for it, until he receive the early and latter rain." Likewise, the divine Husbandman sits at God's right hand in Heaven, and He is waiting for "the precious fruit of the earth." This means that He is waiting until the last soul is saved in order to complete the body of Christ. Then the Man of Patience, who has been tarrying for all these centuries (as we count time on earth), will rise from the throne and "descend from heaven with shout, with the voice of the archangel, and with the trump of God: and the dead in Christ shall rise first: Then we which are alive and remain shall be caught up together with them in the clouds, to meet the Lord in the air: and so shall we ever be with the Lord" (1 Thessalonians 4:16-17).

We need patience as we wait for Him. This patience rests on our realization of the unchanging love of our heavenly Father, so Paul wrote, "The Lord direct your hearts into the love of God" (2 Thessalonians 3:5). What did he mean?

In Jude 21 we find a similar thought: "Keep yourselves in the love of God." What did Jude mean? How can we keep ourselves in the love of God? Are we responsible to keep God loving us? No, for He says, "I have loved thee with an everlasting love" (Jeremiah 31:3). Did Jude mean that we are to keep loving God? No, for 1 John 4:19 says, "We love him, because he first loved us."

The following illustration may help to explain what Paul and Jude meant. Suppose my child has been ill and during dark and murky weather he has to be kept in the house. Then one day the sun shines brightly and the doctor says, "He can go out today for a few hours, but be sure to warn him to keep in the sunshine." So I say to my boy, "Son, you may go out and enjoy yourself, but the doctor says you are to keep in the sunshine." Then the boy asks, "How can I keep the sun shining?" So I explain, "I am not telling you to keep the sun shining; I am telling you to keep in the sunshine." This story, I think, makes clear what is meant by "Keep yourselves in the love of God" and "The Lord direct your hearts into the love of God." We are to keep in the realization of His love, in the constant enjoyment of it.

As we enjoy His love and learn to rely on it, we can wait in patience for the day when all our trials will be ended and the Lord Jesus will come to take us to be forever with Him.

Warning against Idleness (2 Thessalonians 3:6-15)

Evidently the precious truth of the second coming of our Lord had so gripped the hearts of the Thessalonians that they were fully expecting Him to return in their lifetime. I gather from this passage and the corresponding verses in the first Epistle (4:11-12) that some of the members of the church at Thessalonica who did not particularly enjoy hard work were saying, "Well, if the Lord is coming soon, what is the use of working? Why not take it easy? Let those who have enough laid up for the future divide it with us. There is no need to work." The apostle rebuked them and reminded them, "When we were with you, this we commanded you, that if any would not work, neither should he eat" (2 Thessalonians 3:10).

Work may be of one kind or another; it may be mental or physical. But everyone in this world is expected to do work of some kind. God said to Adam, "In the sweat of thy face shalt thou eat bread" (Genesis 3:19). God could provide for us without our working, but it might not be good for us. We benefit physically and intellectually as we use the muscles and minds that God has given us. Professor Henry Van Dyke's lines are thoroughly apropos here: "Heaven is blest with perfect rest, but the blessing of Earth is toil."

The idle men to whom Paul referred were simply ignoring the divine plan, for honest labor has a prominent place in Christianity. Every Christian knows that he is expected to give his best service in return for the remuneration he receives. It is God who has ordained that men should support themselves by their labor.

When men are not employed properly, there is always the danger that they will busy themselves in matters in which they ought not to interfere. They can become nuisances and be used of Satan to disturb the peace of the church or the peace of those to whom they look for their support. The tongue does not offend so seriously when the hands are kept busy.

It is only right to let the idler see that his behavior does not meet with the approval of his fellow Christians (2 Thessalonians 3:14). However, such a person is not to be treated unkindly; he is to be admonished "as a brother" (3:15).

Conclusion (2 Thessalonians 3:16-18)

The last section of three verses gives us the benediction and concluding salutation. Every authentic Epistle written by Paul closes with a similar message about grace. Here he wrote, "The grace of our Lord Jesus Christ be with you all" (3:18). Saved by grace and sustained by grace himself, the apostle ever commended that grace to others.

AUTHOR BIOGRAPHY

HENRY ALLAN IRONSIDE, one of this century's greatest preachers, was born in Toronto, Canada, on October 14, 1876. He lived his life by faith; his needs at crucial moments were met in the most remarkable ways.

Though his classes stopped with grammar school, his fondness for reading and an incredibly retentive memory put learning to use. His scholarship was well recognized in academic circles with Wheaton College awarding an honorary Litt. D. in 1930 and Bob Jones University an honorary D.D. in 1942. Dr. Ironside was also appointed to the boards of numerous Bible institutes, seminaries, and Christian organizations.

"HAI" lived to preach and he did so widely throughout the United States and abroad. E. Schuyler English, in his biography of Ironside, revealed that during 1948, the year HAI was 72, and in spite of failing eyesight, he "gave 569 addresses, besides participating in many other ways." In his eighteen years at Chicago's Moody Memorial Church, his only pastorate, every Sunday but two had at least one profession of faith in Christ.

H. A. Ironside went to be with the Lord on January 15, 1951. Throughout his ministry, he authored expositions on 51 books of the Bible and through the great clarity of his messages led hundreds of thousands, worldwide, to a knowledge of God's Word. His words are as fresh and meaningful today as when first preached.

The official biography of Dr. Ironside, *H. A. Ironside: Ordained of the Lord*, is available from the publisher.

THE WRITTEN MINISTRY OF H. A. IRONSIDE

Expositions

Joshua
Ezra
Nehemiah
Esther
Psalms (1-41 only)
Proverbs
Song of Solomon
Isaiah
Jeremiah
Lamentations
Ezekiel
Daniel
The Minor Prophets
Matthew
Mark
Luke
John

Acts
Romans
1 & 2 Corinthians
Galatians
Ephesians
Philippians
Colossians
1 & 2 Thessalonians
1 & 2 Timothy
Titus
Philemon
Hebrews
James
1 & 2 Peter
1,2, & 3 John
Jude
Revelation

Doctrinal Works

Baptism
Death and Afterward
Eternal Security of the Believer
Holiness: The False and
   the True
The Holy Trinity

Letters to a Roman Catholic
   Priest
The Levitical Offerings
Not Wrath But Rapture
Wrongly Dividing the Word
   of Truth

Historical Works

The Four Hundred Silent Years
A Historical Sketch of the Brethren Movement

Other works by the author are brought back into print from time to time. All of this material is available from your local Christian bookstore or from the publisher.

LOIZEAUX

A Heritage of Ministry . . .

Paul and Timothy Loizeaux began their printing and publishing activities in the farming community of Vinton, Iowa, in 1876. Their tools were rudimentary: a hand press, several fonts of loose type, ink, and a small supply of paper. There was certainly no dream of a thriving commercial enterprise. It was merely the means of supplying the literature needs for their own ministries, with the hope that the Lord would grant a wider circulation. It wasn't a business; it was a ministry.

Our Foundation Is the Word of God

We stand without embarrassment on the great fundamentals of the faith: the inspiration and authority of Scripture, the deity and spotless humanity of our Lord Jesus Christ, His atoning sacrifice and resurrection, the indwelling of the Holy Spirit, the unity of the church, the second coming of the Lord, and the eternal destinies of the saved and lost.

Our Mission Is to Help People Understand God's Word

We are not in the entertainment business. We only publish books and computer software we believe will be of genuine help to God's people, both through the faithful exposition of Scripture and practical application of its principles to contemporary need.

Faithfulness to the Word and consistency in what we publish have been hallmarks of Loizeaux through four generations. And that means when you see the name Loizeaux on the outside, you can trust what is on the inside. That is our promise to the Lord...and to you.

If Paul and Timothy were to visit us today they would still recognize the work they began in 1876. Because some very important things haven't changed at all...this is still a ministry.